毅冰◎著

十天搞定外贸函电

（白金版）

中国海关出版社有限公司
·北京·

图书在版编目（CIP）数据

十天搞定外贸函电：白金版／毅冰著 . —北京：
中国海关出版社有限公司，2019.4
　ISBN　978-7-5175-0347-7

　Ⅰ.①十…　Ⅱ.①毅…　Ⅲ.①对外贸易－英语－电报
信函－写作　Ⅳ.①F75

中国版本图书馆 CIP 数据核字（2019）第 036064 号

十天搞定外贸函电（白金版）
SHITIAN GAODING WAIMAO HANDIAN（BAIJIN BAN）

作　　者：毅　冰
策划编辑：马　超
责任编辑：郭　坤
责任监制：孙　倩
出版发行：中国海关出版社有限公司

社　　址：北京市朝阳区东四环南路甲 1 号　　　　邮政编码：100023
编 辑 部：01065194242－7554（电话）　　　　　　01065194234（传真）
发 行 部：01065194221/4238/4246/4227（电话）　01065194233（传真）
社办书店：01065195616/5127（电话/传真）　　　01065194262/63（邮购电话）
印　　刷：北京华联印刷有限公司　　　　　　　　经　　销：新华书店
开　　本：710mm×1000mm　1/16
印　　张：22.5
字　　数：396 千字
版　　次：2019 年 4 月第 2 版
印　　次：2024 年 10 月第 8 次印刷
书　　号：ISBN　978－7－5175－0347－7
定　　价：69.00 元

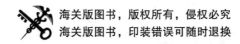

再版序

七年

敲下键盘的时候，已经是二〇一八年的三月，离我最初写作这本书的时间，已经接近七年。七年间，很多事情会发生，很多东西会变化，很多行业会出现，很多产品会消失。这就是自然规律，就是我们中国人所说的"物是人非"，也就是英文的"Things are still there, but the people has changed"。

让我高兴的是，这本书居然可以热卖那么多年，受到一批又一批读者的喜爱，这是对我用心创作的最大鼓励，也是对我工作和思维方式的肯定。

一、七年之变

这七年来，外贸环境在变化，沟通方式在变化，国际主流的邮件写法和思维架构也在变化。过去的商务用词，如今在 Plain English（简易英语）大行其道的环境下，也随之发生了不少变革。现在美国人的邮件写法，跟七年前也有了不小的变化。这些东西，是潜移默化的，是很难通过闭门造车，凭空想出来的，一定要走出去，多看、多交流、多学习、多摸索，总结出一套自己的东西。

这七年来，我从中国到美国，到澳大利亚、新西兰，游历了二十多个国家和地区，亲身经历和见证了商业模式的巨变，很多落后的思维方式、沟通习惯应当扫进废纸堆了。因为时代在变，你的同行在变，你若是依然沉湎过去，用七年前的招数来应对如今的商业环境，恐怕会一败涂地。

二、"电子邮件"

外贸函电这个领域七年间经历巨变，如今"信函"在外贸交流中的比重可以忽略不计，"电子邮件"（简称电邮）成为外贸工作交流的主流媒介。移动端技术的突飞猛进，也应运而生了一大堆移动办公的软件和交流工具，成为主流邮件外的辅助。

我们可以设想一下，如果你坚持传统，坚信经典的力量，在如今的时代还是通过书信的方式，运用二十多年前的外贸手法和思维方式去开发客户，还可能成功吗？别笑，这就是很现实的问题，邮件也是一样，如果你的同行都顺应时代，在这个信息高度扁平化的商业世界里占据一席之地，你能不去改变，不与时俱进吗？

所以，再好的内容，再好的技巧，再好的模式，再好的思维，要想在岁月长河中留存下来，就只能去拥抱变化，去主动改变。你被同行超越，往往不是别人够强，而是你停留在原地，而别人在进步。老业务员感觉到新人的竞争压力，就是这个道理，你十年前的经验，用了十年无变化，而别人或许一上来就用最新的武器，所以攻守之势异也，前浪可能被后浪拍在沙滩上。

三、重新审视我的作品

《十天搞定外贸函电》的第一版，写作的时间是七年前，反映的是七年前的我，书中的思维、遣词、用句，都是七年前的手法。这七年来，这个世界在变化，商业环境在变化，我也在变化，按照如今的眼光去回看，很多内容还是略显稚嫩了。

四、我到底都改了什么

相比第一版，我修改了大约50%的内容，包括重新梳理体例，增加了Outline（提纲挈领）模块；重新编写或更新部分邮件，让电邮内容和写作手法更加与时俱进；优化 More Expressions（触类旁通）中的部分句型，使其更加贴近外贸人的实际工作。此外，我还对全书进行了勘误。

七年后，我重新审阅、修订这本书，希望给大家呈现一个七年后的我，一个思维更缜密，邮件写作手法更老到的我，希望大家在学习的过程中，能感受到不一样的气场。此外，我还希望，在接下来的七年里，这本白金版的《十天搞定外贸函电》，能继续引领外贸邮件潮流，继续占据这个专业领域的畅销书榜。

我有充分信心，你呢?

毅　冰

2018 年 3 月 15 日于新西兰皇后镇

序

不走寻常路，十天写一手漂亮的电子邮件

恭喜你，我的朋友！你手上正拿着一本非常重要的书，通过这十天的阅读，相信你的英文函电写作能力一定会有意想不到的提高。除此之外，也能让你的同事、供应商、客户明显感受到你的专业素养和工作能力的提升，助你赢得订单，获得升迁，争取更好的工作机会。

一、最简单、地道的英文表达，让你彻底告别传统函电

如果这时候，你还在苦学着传统的函电教材，还在皱着眉头背诵、默写着各种范文和例句，那就把这本书拿来看看，不需要用整块的时间来研读，也不需要做太多的笔记、查太多的生词，只需轻松地翻阅，便可找到自己需要的东西，写一手漂亮的 E-mail。

当然，如果你已经习惯了传统的商务信函书写，不喜欢简洁的句型、地道的用法和口语化的英文表达，那也可以转送给朋友，或者拿来垫垫桌脚。但是，如果真想学学地道的英文表达、英美人士的邮件书写习惯、母语人士的思维方式，学会如何用最简单的单词和句子来应付工作中的各类问题，那么本书绝对值得一读。

外贸函电其实不用那么沉闷，可以很灵活、很形象、很简单地表达自己的想法。"沟通"才是邮件的核心与关键。过去的商务信函，侧重于"正式表达"，内容要得体，表达要清楚、详细，用词要符合商务用语的规范。可时代在变，函电也不再是过去的函电，"函"越来越少，"电"越来越频繁，电邮

在很大程度上替代了原有的书信和传真，而"简洁""明白""准确"的函电，已成了当今的主流。

二、掌握最新 KISS 原则，快速走出思维误区

如今的英文邮件书写，可以用 KISS 这个词来形容。拆开四个字母，就变成"Keep it short and simple"，中文含义是保持简洁、简单。也有朋友理解为"Keep it stupid and simple"，这就更形象了。用最简单的话来写邮件，对方能看不懂吗？

写邮件的目的是"沟通"，为实际工作服务，而不是卖弄英文水平。对专业的商务人士而言，每天要处理很多事情、很多邮件，没有时间阅读长篇大论的东西。不耽误彼此时间，长话短说，用最简单的词、最简单的句子，让对方准确理解要表达的内容，真正做到"惜字如金"，那就出师了。

三、外贸全流程函电一网打尽

为了让朋友们快速上手，在短期内迅速了解到当前主流英文邮件的写法，笔者将外贸工作中可能发生的数百种情况，根据工作的流程和进展，大致归纳为九天学习，分别为前期联络、开发信的书写、询盘的处理、报价和跟进的方法，还有谈判、装运、验货、验厂、收款等，详解不同情境和语境下的邮件书写，让读者阅读后在实际工作中可以"脱笔而出"。而第十天，专门讲解细节问题，供学有余力的朋友总结和提高。

四、秘而不宣的外贸知识点无私分享

本书在每章的各个小节后，增加了可替代的例句，尽量覆盖工作的方方面面，应付一些突如其来的问题。另外还专门设置了"Useful Tips（零敲碎打）"章节，每节阐述一个外贸小知识，介绍一些笔者认为特别重要的细节，或者平时网络中不太能搜到，但工作中必不可少的要点，让你在收获函电精华的同时，学到更多的外贸技能。

五、外贸函电确实如此简单

事实上，函电就是这么简单！不需要太高的英文水平，不需要太多的词汇，你也可以把邮件写得这么自信，这么优雅，这么随意，使一手漂亮的邮件成为你工作中的亮点。

最后，衷心感谢中国海关出版社对我的信任，以及马超编辑对于本书写作提出的宝贵意见。还要感谢 Steven、Ashley、Bush、Justin、Jason、空谷幽兰等朋友给予的支持、建议和许多想法。此外，还要感谢诸位读者朋友对于本书出版的殷切期待，有了你们，才有了本书的问世。

是为序。

毅 冰

2011 年 7 月 30 日

于香港中环 Café Landmark

目录 Contents

第一天

前期联络
Pre-business Contact

1 邀请客户见面 Requesting Business Appointment

谈生意，最有效的方式莫过于面对面交流，这样做可以使双方更加容易拉近彼此的距离，不会显得过分冰冷。适时邀请客户面谈，是业务开发和跟进的一个重要环节。

Meeting at Canton Fair

To : Michael Peterson

Cc :

Bcc :

From : Peter Liang

Subject : Meeting at Canton Fair

Signature: Apple Mail!

Dear Michael,

Glad to meet you at Canton Fair！ We're pleased to know that you plan to visit Shanghai next week.

If possible, please go and see our factory with a field inspection then. Your interested items will be set up in the showroom for your review.

Looking forward to your early reply！

Regards,

Peter

Outline（提纲挈领）

1. 在某个展会，介词要用 at 而不是 in。比如在广交会，就是 at Canton Fair，在香港展，就是 at HK Fair。

2. go and see our factory：走访我们工厂。

3. field inspection：实地考察。在这里，inspection 并没有表示"验货"的含义。

4. set up：表示"到位""放置好"。

5. showroom：样品间、陈列室。尽量避免用 sample room 来表达。

More Expressions（触类旁通）

1. Glad to meet/see you at Tools & Hardware Fair.
很高兴在五金工具展上跟您见面。

2. Are you going to China in the near future？
您最近会来中国吗？

3. What about your schedule？
您的行程如何安排？

4. I'm not sure if it would be convenient for you to visit our company next week.
我不确定您下周是否方便来我们公司。

5. The items which you selected in our booth will be collected in our showroom.
我们会把您在我们展位上挑选的东西都集中到样品间。

Q&A（深入浅出）

Question：
邮件写作时是否一定要在称呼前加 Dear？

Answer：

其实未必，商务邮件的写作，这么多年来其实变化很大。原先正式化、公式化的邮件写法，如今已经变得更加口语化和生活化。人与人之间的距离，相对而言会拉近许多，不再是过去那种一板一眼的刻板表述，遣词造句变得十分灵活。

Dear 的用法相对正式，作为尊称用于称呼新客户，或者职位比较高或者年龄比较大的老客户较为合适。比如 Dear Monica, Dear Mr. Peterson, Dear Dr. Garfield，都是标准的用法，不容易让人产生误会。可如果跟客户已经很熟悉，有多年的交情，又或者都是同龄人，直呼其名也未尝不可。

当然，偶尔也可以在名字前加上 Hi 或者 Hello 之类的口语化用词，也会给客户一点小小的温暖。比如 Hi Nancy 这种打招呼的方式，就好比人与人之间面对面打招呼，从文字中投射出会话场景，显得亲近和自然。

2 讨论时间地点 Scheduling Visiting Itinerary

一旦客户确定来访，必须事先确认好时间和地点，并安排好来回行程和车辆等。把可以考虑到的细节，都尽量做完美，争取给客户留下专业的印象。

Preparing itinerary

To：Michael Peterson

Cc：

Bcc：

From：Peter Liang

Subject：Preparing itinerary

Signature: Apple Mail! ◇

Dear Michael,

Thanks a lot for your prompt reply. It is acceptable for us on 2nd Feb.

Could you please advise your flight number？ We will arrange the pick up at Shanghai Pudong airport and drive you to Mandarin Oriental Hotel after meeting.

Kindly let me know if any change about your trip.

Thanks and best regards,
Peter

Outline（提纲挈领）

1. prompt reply：快速的回复，相当于 quick reply。

2. acceptable：可以接受的，没问题的。这里也可以用 available 替代。

3. flight number：航班号。接送客户最重要的是了解对方具体的航班号，这样可以时时关注和留意航班信息，比如是否有延误，或者什么时候到，在哪个航站楼等相关信息，以便提早做出安排。

4. Mandarin Oriental Hotel：文华东方酒店，国际著名的酒店，由香港总部管理整个集团的全球酒店业务。

5. kindly：友善地、亲切地，在这里用作副词。kindly let me know，基本接近于 please let me know，是邮件中的常用表达。

 More Expressions（触类旁通）

1. Thank you/Thanks for your prompt reply/response.

感谢您的及时回复。

2. Could you kindly advise your itinerary？

能否麻烦告知我您的行程安排？

3. Please keep me posted on this！

请让我知道（这件事的）最新进展！

4. I'm sorry but my boss is only available next Tuesday.

抱歉，我老板只有下周二才有空。

5. Is it acceptable to pick you up at 8：30 a.m.？ In the lobby？

早上八点半来接您可以吗？在酒店大堂见？

⊕ Q&A（深入浅出）

Question：

商务邮件怎样分段落才专业？

Answer：

一般来说，商务邮件的写作要遵循 3C 基本原则，也就是 Clearness（清楚），Conciseness（简洁）和 Courtesy（礼貌）。邮件不仅要有条理，而且不能太差，更不能生涩难懂。要把复杂的事情做归纳和梳理，用简单的句型有条理、有逻辑性地表达出来，让看的人不觉得疲惫，一眼扫过去就能明白你想说的内容，这才是我们学习邮件写作的要点和方向。

我觉得，邮件除了称呼和落款，大部分的正文内容尽量控制在 3~4 段，也就是我常说的三段式写法和四段式写法。"橄榄球"型结构，上下略短，中间丰满，核心内容在中间段突出，这种写法比较符合国际惯例，也较常用，符合视觉审美。

3 取消本次会面 Cancelling The Meeting

很多时候，客户的行程会根据具体情况的变化而变化。修改时间，修改地点，甚至取消某场或者某几场会面，都是时有发生的。

Cancelling the meeting

To : Peter Liang

Cc :

Bcc :

From : Michael Peterson

Subject : Cancelling the meeting

Signature: Apple Mail!

Peter,

As I have another big talk in Hong Kong, I won't drop in on you during the buying trip.

Maybe next time. And sorry for the inconvenience of you guys.

Sincerely,
Michael

Outline（提纲挈领）

1. big talk：重要的会议，这里是口语化的用法，相当于 important meeting。

2. drop in：顺便拜访，后面跟 on somebody。

3. buying trip：采购行程。

4. inconvenience：不便，是 inconvenient 的名词形式。

5. you guys：你们，相比单独用一个词 you，you guys 显得更加口语化，更亲切和随意，像老朋友之间的交流。

More Expressions（触类旁通）

1. Please help to cancel my hotel booking.
麻烦你帮我取消酒店的预订。

2. Kindly check the attached scanned copy of my passport.
请看附件，关于我护照的扫描件。

3. Sorry to inform you that I have to cancel this buying trip.
抱歉通知你，我不得不取消这次采购行程。

4. Hope to see you ASAP.
希望能尽快见到您。

5. Please accept my apology.
请接受我的道歉。

Q&A（深入浅出）

Question：
ASAP 是什么意思？

Answer：

ASAP 是 as soon as possible 的首字母缩写，表示"尽快"。邮件力求简洁，自然而然就出现了很多常用的缩写。

比如 FYI 表示 for your information（供您参考），ETD 表示 estimated time of departure（预计开船日），ETA 表示 estimated time of arrival（预计到达日），APPROX 表示 approximately（大约），CBM 表示 cubic meter（立方米）等，这类缩写还有很多。

4 见面后的跟进 Follow-up After Meeting

跟客户面谈过后，高效地跟进是十分必要的。一方面唤起客户的记忆，另一方面展示自己的专业和效率。

Meeting recap

To : John Stuart

Cc :

Bcc :

From : Stanley Yang

Subject : Meeting recap

Signature: Apple Mail!

Dear Dr.Stuart,

According to your selection in the meeting this morning, we're now preparing the offer sheet in detail. And you will get received in 3 days.

Best regards,
Stanley

Outline（提纲挈领）

1. Dr. Stuart：斯图亚特博士。在英文中，如果对方的名片上印有 PHD（博士）的字样，那对于客户就需要特别用到尊称，不能用 Mr. Stuart，而要改用 Dr. Stuart，以表尊敬。

2. offer sheet：报价单，也可以写成 quote sheet 或者 quotation sheet。

3. in detail：详细地。

4. get received：收到，这里用被动语态。

5. in 3 days：三天内。

More Expressions（触类旁通）

1. Please find the offer sheet in attachment.
请看附件中的报价单。

2. I'm sorry we don't have the exact same model.
抱歉，我们没有完全一样的产品。

3. We could provide a similar item for your reference.
我们可以提供一款类似的产品供您参考。

4. We're pretty familiar with the US market.
我们对美国市场非常了解。

5. The items which you had interest were already sent to your office.
您选中的产品我们都已经寄往您的公司了。

Q&A（深入浅出）

Question：
跟客户见面后，隔多久跟进比较合适？

Answer：

要根据实际情况来分析。如果客户仅仅是初次拜访，大致了解了你们的公司和产品，但并未针对具体的产品索要报价或样品，那三五天后跟进，简单表示对客户拜访的感谢，介绍自己的产品，顺便推荐一些热卖的款式，并且大致展示其优势和特点，基本上就差不多了。

如果客户选定了某些样品并要求报价，那最好当天或者第二天就给客户一个准确的答复。就算暂时无法提供详细报价单，也要做一个 offer recap（报价综述），插入图片、简单描述和价格，做成一个表格，先给客户过目。等准确的外箱资料、测试要求等资料齐全后，再将其他信息补充完整，做成详细的报价单继续跟进。

总而言之，时间不宜拖得太久，最好一周内就解决这些问题，在最佳时间段完成跟进的重要步骤。

5 展会后的联络 Contacting After Fairs

展会过后，必须第一时间跟进客户，而且要给客户提供相关信息，让客户能够回忆起当时的场景。即便客户无法准确记起谈判的细节，也要给对方丰富的资料，引起对方兴趣，为后续的谈判做铺垫。

Quotes for hand tool kit

To : Catty Willing

Cc :

Bcc :

From : Arthur Kwan

Subject : Quotes for hand tool kit

Signature: Apple Mail!

Dear Catty,

Thank you for visiting our booth at Spoga Fair in Cologne.

According to your selection for hand tool kit, please help to check the photos with offer recap in attachment.

I'm now working on the packaging info with my colleagues, and will send you the quotes in detail asap.

Furthermore, the testing report will be sent out in separate email.

Best regards,
Arthur

Outline（提纲挈领）

1. Spoga Fair：德国工具类展会，每年在科隆举行。
2. Cologne：科隆，德国城市，德语拼写是 Köln。
3. hand tool kit：手工具套装。
4. packaging info：包装信息。
5. separate email：另一封邮件。

More Expressions（触类旁通）

1. We supply power tools to EU market.

我们出口电动工具到欧盟市场。

2. I would like to recommend you some new items matching the Scandinavian market.

我想推荐一些适合北欧市场的新产品给您。

3. The offer sheet will be sent to you in separate email.

我会通过另一封邮件把报价单发给您。

4. All of our products are strictly according to DIN standard of Germany.

我们的产品完全符合德国 DIN 工具类标准。

5. If you have buying trip after this Canton Fair, please advise us of your time schedule. Welcome to visit our showroom in Guangzhou then.

如果您在广交会后有采购行程，麻烦您告知我们具体的计划。届时非常欢迎您走访我们在广州的样品间。

Q&A（深入浅出）

Question：

为什么广交会要翻译成 Canton Fair，而不是 Guangzhou Fair？

Answer：

事实上，我们通过广交会的官方网站（www.cantonfair.org.cn）就可以发现，官方的准确表达应该是"中国进出口商品交易会"，对应的英文翻译是 China Import & Export Fair。而 Canton 是"广州"的旧式翻译，国外习惯使用这个词。因为"中国进出口商品交易会"每年在广州举行，所以 Canton Fair 就逐渐变成了一种约定俗成的固定搭配。只要一说起 Canton Fair，别人就明白是广交会。

其实很多旧式翻译，因为被广泛应用，一直沿用至今。比如清华还是习惯被翻译成 Tsinghua。比如北京，很多时候还是习惯被翻译成 Peking。林语堂先生的名著《京华烟云》，原书的名字就是 *Moment in Peking*。

只要平时多留意，就会发现这类翻译还有很多。

6 开发潜在客户 Developing Potential Customers

　　业务员平时的工作中，除了服务老客户以外，难免需要花大量的时间来培养和开发新客户。所以日常写的邮件，一部分是回复询盘和处理各种事宜，还有一部分，就是写给陌生客户寻找商机的。这一部分，就是我们所谓的"开发信"了。

Hand tool supplier with good quality & certified reports

To : Judy White

Cc :

Bcc :

From : Shirley Cheng

Subject : Hand tool supplier with good quality & certified reports

Signature: Apple Mail!

Dear Judy,

Glad to get your email address online.
We supply all kinds of hand tools to global market with good quality and reasonable price. And our items are strictly according to ANSI, BS, DIN, NF & JIS tool standards.

As per my surfing on your official website, I found that you have some chain stores in Europe, US and Japan. It is our pleasure to find a way to cooperate with you, if possible.

Here attached are some photos for our showroom and

some hot-selling items for your reference. And I will send you the offer sheet, testing report & factory audit report in separate emails soon.

Best regards,
Shirley Cheng

Outline（提纲挈领）

1. reasonable price：合适的价格。很多时候，我们无须一味强调价格低，其实很多客户也明白一分价钱一分货的道理。所以"可靠的价格"，往往能让人联想到"可靠的供应商"。

2. surfing：冲浪，是 surf 的 ing 形式。浏览网站，可以形象地表达为"网上冲浪"。

3. official website：官方网站。

4. chain stores：连锁店。

5. hot-selling items：热卖产品，也可以用 top-rated items 来替代。

More Expressions（触类旁通）

1. We supply plastic bottles to Japan with good quality and competitive price.
我们的塑料水瓶出口日本，品质不错且价格有竞争力。

2. Attached are some photos for your review, for our unique star items.
附上一些图片供您参考，都是我们独特的明星产品。

3. Free samples could be sent on request.
我们可以根据您的要求提供免费样品。

4. Nice and solid packaging is our advantage.

美观且结实耐用的包装是我们的卖点。

5. The 3rd party factory audit report and testing report will be sent for your approval soon.

第三方的验厂报告和测试报告会尽快发给您确认。

 Q&A（深入浅出）

Question：

ANSI, BS, DIN, NF & JIS tool standards 分别指什么？

Answer：

这是不同国家对于工具行业的相关标准，具体如下：

ANSI tool standard：美国工具标准（ANSI 是 American National Standards Institute 的简写）；

BS tool standard：英国工具标准（BS 指 British Standard 的简写）；

DIN tool standard：德国工具标准（DIN 是德语 Deutsches Institut für Normung 的简写，翻译成英文就是 German Institute for Standardlization）；

NF tool standard：法国工具标准（NF 是法语 Association Française de Normalisation 的简写，就是法国标准化协会）；

JIS tool standard：日本工具标准（JIS 是 Japanese Industrial Standard 的简写）。

7 介绍自己的优势 Introducing Our Advantages

开发潜在客户和新客户，很重要的一点就是要吸引对方注意，让对方觉得跟你合作能各取所需。除了适当地推销自己外，你还需要让客户知道你们公司和产品的优势和特点。简言之，就是要突出 selling point（卖点）。

Advantages & testing report

To : Judy White

Cc :

Bcc :

From : Shirley Cheng

Subject : Advantages & testing report

Signature: Apple Mail!

Judy,

Please get the 3rd party testing report as attached. We have full confidence in achieving your quality level.

By the way, here are the brief introduction of our advantages as follows:

1. Cooperation with a majority of importers in the US for more than 8 years

2. Experience in doing business with heavy customers

---

3. Delivery time control for decent orders

4. Designing team for new products development

5. Factory audit report by SGS, Intertek & Wal-Mart

6. Free samples for customers

Any further questions, please do not hesitate to contact me.

Best regards,

Shirley Cheng

Outline（提纲挈领）

1. quality level：质量标准。

2. brief introduction：简要介绍。

3. a majority of：大量的，可以用来替代常用的 a lot of。

4. heavy customer：大客户、大买家。

5. decent order：正式订单。

More Expressions（触类旁通）

1. We have a professional R&D team.

我们有专业的市场调研和研发部门。

2. Firstly, I'd like to introduce our advantages in short.

首先，我想简单介绍一下我们的优势所在。

3. This is our unique and patented product.

这是我们独一无二的产品，且拥有专利。

4. We have full confidence in getting the UL certificate.

我们有充分信心能拿到美国 UL 认证。

5. The stable delivery time is one of our advantages.

稳定的交货期是我们公司的一项重要优势。

 Q&A（深入浅出）

Question：

R&D 具体指什么？为什么很多外企有这样的岗位和部门？

Answer：

R&D 的全称是 Research & Development，指市场调研与开发。其实在欧美的许多公司都有相关的部门和专业的团队开展市场调研和开发。一般要切入新的市场，开发新的客户，或者对某一类产品进行相关研究和背景调查，以便做垂直领域的细分客户，都少不了这方面的工作。

一个以出口产品为主要业务的公司，必须对海外市场和目标区域市场相当了解。如果你要把产品销往美国，可公司对美国的市场情况和政策法规一无所知，那如何能做出让美国进口商信赖，让美国消费者喜欢的产品呢？

根据笔者的海外工作经验，也有部分客户把 R&D 里面的 D，理解成 Design，那就把 R&D 理解成了"调研与设计"，这种理解就更近了一步，不仅要了解目标市场，更要迎合目标客户，更加突出自己的设计特色，并将其打造为核心竞争力。

8 突出专业素养 Highlighting Specialties

　　与客户的前期接触，不仅是询价、报价这么简单，那只是新手刚入门时所处的初级阶段的情况而已。对于老业务员而言，需要做的事更多，更上一个层次，以体现自身的专业素养，增强潜在客户和目标客户跟你合作的信心。只要让对方觉得你是"行家"，他找你谈是找对人了，前期的目的就达到了。

Suggestions for OEM orders

To : Judy White

Cc :

Bcc :

From : Shirley Cheng

Subject : Suggestions for OEM orders

Signature: Apple Mail!

Dear Judy,

Thank you so much for your quick response with constructive suggestions. The delivery time for manufacturing 3,000 sets of tool kits in your brand is 30-40 days after the order is confirmed. In fact, it is no problem for us to handle OEM orders. However, we have other 2 options below for your consideration to save the cost.

Option 1：
Please add the quantity to 4,000 sets to fill in a full 40'FCL.

The freight cost for each set will be cheaper than LCL shipment. By the way, as I mentioned in the offer sheet, the MOQ for each item with OEM is one 40 feet container, or we have to charge 200USD as handling cost.

Option 2：

If you'd like to keep the previous quantity with no update, we suggest you run this order in our brand and current packaging for cost saving. There is no handling charge, film charge or other extra cost. And the delivery time will be shortened to 20 days.

Kindly check and advise your comments to proceed. Thanks.

Best regards,
Shirley Cheng

Outline（提纲挈领）

1. response：回复，相当于 reply，可以交替使用。

2. for your consideration：供您参考，跟 for your review 或 for your reference 接近。

3. FCL：整柜，是 full container loading 的首字母缩写。

4. LCL：散货，是 less than full container loading 的首字母缩写。

5. film charge：制版费。

 More Expressions（触类旁通）

1. We have experience in handling OEM orders.

我们有操作贴牌订单生产的经验。

2. I'm afraid you have to pay for JPY30,000 as handling charge, because your quantity hasn't reached our MOQ.

恐怕我们要向您收取 3 万日元的操作费，因为订单没有达到我们的最小起订量。

3. It is better for us to handle the full container orders.

对我们而言，操作整柜的订单更好。

4. Please find our other suggestions as follows.

请看下面我们的一些其他建议。

5. It takes more than 45 days for doing orders in your packaging.

如果订单要按照您的包装来做，那需要 45 天以上的时间。

 Q&A（深入浅出）

Question：

OEM 和 ODM 具体指什么？有什么区别？

Answer：

OEM 是英文 Original Equipment Manufacturer 的首字母缩写，是指供应商按照客户的委托生产，仅仅只是"生产加工"，而产品的要求、包装、设计等，都是客户提供的。目前国内的出口型企业，很多还是停留在 OEM 的阶段，自主研发、创新、设计和品牌塑造的能力还不强。

ODM 有所不同，是英文 Original Design Manufacturer 的首字母缩写，是指原始设计厂商。如果一个供应商有 Design（设计）的能力，就不会在供应链的底端做简单的加工生产，而会往其他环节切入，去打开终端市场。比如联想的 Thinkpad 笔记本、华为的路由器和手机类产品，都是自己研发、自己生产、自己设计的，是典型的 ODM。

对于大多数企业而言，进军海外市场，往往都从 OEM 开始，慢慢接触和试水，总结经验和试错，做好 R&D 以后，才逐渐往 ODM 过渡。这是一个艰难的过程，但是，也是中国外贸人必须走的路。

第二天

商务往来
Running Business

Part 1　询盘处理 Dealing With Inquiries

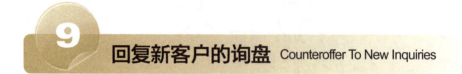

9　回复新客户的询盘 Counteroffer To New Inquiries

收到询盘后，就应该仔细研究，并在第一时间给予客户回复，切不可拖沓，因为很多机会，都是在等待中失去的。效率，往往会成为业务开发的关键。

Offer sheet provided soon

To : Abby Jansen

Cc :

Bcc :

From : Scott Wang

Subject : Offer sheet provided soon

Signature: Apple Mail!

Dear Abby,

So pleased to receive your inquiry from our official website.

We're one of the leading vendors for mobile components in Greater China Region. And our factory is strictly in terms of ISO9001 for manufacturing high-

---

quality & reliable products.

I just transferred your email to my manager, and he would provide you with our latest offer sheet soon.

Kind regards,
Scott Wang

Outline（提纲挈领）

1. vendor：供应商，跟 supplier 含义接近。

2. mobile components：手机配件。

3. Greater China Region：一般用于指代中国大陆和港澳台地区。也有部分跨国公司，把以华人为主的新加坡，也归类在这个市场。

4. in terms of：根据，按照，与 according to 可以替换使用。

5. transfer：转让，转移，转发，可转让信用证，就是 transferrable L/C。

More Expressions（触类旁通）

1. Very pleased to get your inquiry through HKTDC.com.
很高兴通过香港贸易发展局网站收到您的询盘。

2. I have to check with my supplier about the updated price.
我需要跟我的供应商确认一下新的价格。

3. The quotation sheet will be provided no later than this Friday.
报价单会在本周五之前发给您。

4. Please inform us of your contact info for receiving the hard copy of price list.
请提供一下您的联系方式，我们会把报价单打印好快递给您。

5. Would you like to have a look at our catalogues ?

您想要看一下我们的产品样本吗？

 Q&A（深入浅出）

Question :

要不要给新接触的潜在客户寄样本？是否应该询问到付账号？

Answer :

样本是公司主要的对外展示产品的媒介，能够起到橱窗的作用，给客户展示现有的产品，引起对方的兴趣和购买欲望。这跟各大超市卖场印刷分发的广告页是一个道理，就是让消费者拿在手里，前前后后翻看一下，多少会对某些产品有一些意向。

可样本毕竟是样本，不是客户索要的样品。根据国际惯例，单独给客户快递样本，是需要由供应商承担相关费用的。除非客户主动要求到付，否则询问客户到付账号并不合适。

出于成本和环保因素的考虑，如今 PDF 或者 PPT 形式的 e-catalogue（电子样本）逐渐流行起来。只需要通过邮件发送即可，免去了高昂的快递费，而且大大节约了时间。这里有一点需要注意，发送邮件前一定要控制好文件的大小，5M 以内的文件我个人觉得比较合适。

如果文件特别大，那就建议通过其他的在线传输工具来处理。

10 回复有针对性的询盘 Counteroffer To Specific Inquiries

做久了业务的人都会知道，有针对性的询盘一般情况下质量会高一些，它往往代表了客户的直接需求和购买欲望。泛泛地浏览和精细地询问，是两个不同的概念。客户针对某一产品具体询价，甚至给出了要求、图片及相关信息，必然希望能够在第一时间得到准确翔实的回复。

若这一关能做好，必将在潜移默化中，给客户营造一个专业的第一印象。

Quotes for 200W Power Inverter

To : Rocky Lee

Cc :

Bcc :

From : Hugo Li

Subject : Quotes for 200W Power Inverter

Signature: Apple Mail!

Dear Mr.Lee,

Very glad to see you at Canton Fair yesterday !

Concerning your inquired item#TD-JIC2685, please help to check our offer as follows.

Item: 200W Power Inverter
Article No.: TD-JIC2685
Spec: Could power a variety of electronic products with safe operation

Certificate & testing report: ETL
Packaging: Color box
Packaging size: 15.8"x7.8"x2.4"
Weight: 2.3 lbs
FOB price： USD6.92/pc

Samples could be prepared in 5 working days. Should you have interest in samples evaluation, please send me your address in detail with courier account.

We look forward to your reply soon.

Best regards,
Hugo

Outline（提纲挈领）

1. power inverter：逆变器。

2. as follows：如下。

3. a variety of：大量的。

4. lbs：英制单位"磅"，一磅约等于 454 克。

5. courier account：快递账号。在外贸行业里，一般问对方要快递账号，往往就表示让对方提供"到付账号"，相当于 freight collect（运费到付）。

More Expressions（触类旁通）

1. Concerning your inquired luggage bag, please help to check our quotes

enclosed.

关于您询价的行李包，请看附件的报价单。

2. Please get our updated price list for our beauty cases in attachment.

关于我公司化妆箱的价格，请看附件最新的报价单。

3. Samples will be finished within this week.

样品会在本周内完成。

4. All our products are LFGB certified.

我们所有的产品都通过德国食品级 LFGB 的认证。

5. Would you like to evaluate samples in advance？

你想先看一下样品吗？

 Q&A（深入浅出）

Question：

到付账号如何用英文准确表达？

Answer：

事实上，在写邮件的时候，要尽量避免直译，以免造成语义上的生硬。要尽量符合欧美人士的英文思维，遣词造句要贴近他们的使用习惯。一般而言，索要到付账号大多数是为了给新客户寄样品，此时可以有以下几种表达方式。

1. Freight collect，指运费到付。这是最正统也是最正式的表达方式。如："We accept to send you free samples with freight collect. Please advise your account."（我们同意提供免费样品，但运费需要到付。请提供您的账号。）这里，账号指的就是"到付账号"。因为有上下文，客户可以准确理解具体的内容，不会产生误会。

2. Courier account，指快递账号。这个用法比较地道，是 native speaker（把英语作为母语的人士）习惯使用的。因为如今的邮件写法，已经大异于十几二十年前，越来越偏向口语化，太过正式的用词，反而在欧美人士的邮件里不太常见。关于"请提供一下到付账号"，非常地道的表达就是"Please help

to give us your courier account."

3. Express account, Freight collect account 之类的表达也经常出现在各种邮件里，表示"到付账号"。对于很多并非将英语作为母语的客户而言，太地道的英文反而不容易理解。比如大多数日本客户英文都不太好，一个地道的 courier account，对方或许就不明白。这时，来一句更加直接的："Please give me your FedEx or UPS express account."（请提供一下您的联邦快递或者联合包裹的账号。）会让对方立刻明白你想要表达的含义。

11 回复语焉不详的询盘 Counteroffer To Non-specific Inquiries

很多时候，语焉不详的询盘并非代表询盘质量差，或者客户只是随便问问，也许这是一个不错的机会。每个人的习惯不同，有人喜欢长篇大论，有人喜欢言简意赅，有人喜欢跟供应商详细探讨，有人喜欢根据供应商的推荐来选择产品，不能用经验主义判断客户，对各类客户的询盘不能一概而论。

对于语焉不详的询盘，要找到恰当的切入点和突破口，争取通过专业、高效的回复来赢得客户。

Company profile & main products category

To : Sally Lapsing

Cc :

Bcc :

From : Spencer Ding

Subject : Company profile & main products category

Signature: Apple Mail!

Dear Sally,

Thanks for your kind inquiry！

Frankly speaking, we're a trading company exporting a wide range of products. Here are our main categories below：

1. Hand tool & power tool

2. Art & craft

3. Home textile

4. Sporting accessories

5. Outdoor décor

6. Home use glassware

Please check our company profile as attached. If any interest, we're willing to offer you best price on request.

Best regards,
Spencer Ding

 Outline（提纲挈领）

1. frankly speaking：坦白地说，也可以用 to be candid with you，异曲同工。

2. a wide range of products：很广的产品线。

3. main categories：主要类别。

4. outdoor décor：户外装饰品。décor 是法语外来词，相当于英文的 decoration。

5. be willing to do something：愿意做某事。

 More Expressions（触类旁通）

1. We mainly supply home textile items to the UK.
我们主要供应纺织类产品到英国。

2. Sorry, we're not a manufacturer.
抱歉，我们不是生产商。

3. No need for any quotation at the moment.

目前不需要报价。

4. Attached the photos of wooden items for your selection.

附件是我们的木制品图片，供您选择。

5. What is your core business category？

你们主要做什么产品？

Q&A（深入浅出）

Question：

什么是 company profile（公司简介）？

Answer：

作为一个专业的企业，不管是贸易公司还是工厂，都应该有突出自身形象的东西，能让客户对你的优势和公司情况、业务情况等一目了然。一份好的公司简介，应该图文并茂，并有数据和图表支持，能够增强客户与自己合作的信心。

公司简介可以做成 pdf 或者 ppt 形式，控制图片大小，尽量使整个文件不要过大，便于通过电子邮件来收发。

公司简介是公司对外的形象展示，特别是对于新客户和潜在客户，更加马虎不得。有些专业客户和大买家会主动索取相关信息，也有客户会直接要求供应商填写详细的 vendor profile（供应商登记表），尤其是大客户，一定会注重合作供应商的整体情况和软实力。比如，这个供应商现有的合作客户、每年的销售额、主要的市场、核心的产品、公司成立时间、现有员工人数，是否拥有自己的设计团队和质检部门等，都是值得重点关注的。

个人观点，一份好的公司简介，至少要包含以下内容：

1.公司名称、地址、网址、公司简介。

2.公司图片。

3.样品间图片、产品图片。

4.产品种类及具体介绍。

5. 公司近三年内的销售额（有图表更佳）。

6. 现有的客户分布（有图表更佳）。

7. 现有的主要客户。最好是文字加图形，更容易给对方直观印象，比如公司主要的四个客户分别是 Walmart, Home Depot, Costco, Kroger，就完全可以用图 2-1 的图标来表示，这比苍白的文字更有说服力。

图 2-1

8. 员工人数和职责分类，比如销售团队多少人、质检部门多少人、管理层多少人、设计师多少人、采购跟单多少人等。

9. 如果是工厂，就需要进一步说明现有的生产设备、工人数量、流水线情况、工厂产能、品质控制能力、相关 ISO 标准，还有第三方验厂报告等。

一旦有客户前来公司拜访，就可以打开这个文件，用手提电脑或者 iPad 给客户做一个简单的 presentation（演示），如果有投影仪就更好，可以在会议室或样品间给客户来一场几分钟的专业讲解和分析，能给公司形象加很多印象分。

12 跟进老客户的询价 Inquiry Follow-up For Current Customer

　　给老客户发送邮件时我们往往会非常随意。两个人之间的沟通，不会如陌生人般距离遥远。遣词用句过分客气，反而会显得疏远。用简单的几句话，点明主旨，该说的事情都说到位，不啰唆，不浪费对方时间，这就够了。

Quotes dated on Apr. 3rd

To : Celina Shaman

Cc :

Bcc :

From : Millie Chen

Subject : Quotes dated on Apr. 3rd

Signature: Apple Mail!

Celina,

Have you got my quotes dated on Apr.3rd？ Any comments or feedback from your customer？ If the pricing too high, we could do some changes to reduce the cost.

Plus, I'm going to attend the Canton Fair phase 1 next week. And my assistant will send you our booth number later.

We look forward to your early reply.

Millie

Outline（提纲挈领）

1. quotes dated on Apr.3rd：4 月 3 日的报价。

2. pricing：报价，是 price 的 ing 形式，侧重报价这个动作。

3. plus：它的用法跟 and 类似，承上启下，表示"还有"。

4. Canton Fair phase 1：广交会一期。

5. booth number：摊位号。

 More Expressions（触类旁通）

1. This is out of our target price.

这超出了我们的目标价。

2. Perhaps we could work something out.

也许我们能找到解决办法。

3. We would like to offer up a compromise to get this order.

我们可以做出适当让步来赢得订单。

4. I think we have to do some changes to reduce the cost.

我觉得我们需要做一些改动来降低成本。

5. Rest assured, it is absolutely our best offer.

放心，这绝对是我们最好的价格！

 Q&A（深入浅出）

Question：

能否在收到询盘时就询问目标价？

Answer：

笔者的个人建议是否定的。很多时候客户在询问某类产品时，心里其实并没有底，也许是在国外看到同行在卖，也想试试看，所以才会有询价出现。这个时候，客户往往不会轻易透露底线，因为他自己都不知道底线在哪里，所以，他可能就不回复，那你就失去了一个宝贵的机会，也有可能他会胡乱砍一下价格，那对供应商更加不利。

　　跟老客户之间沟通，彼此知根知底，偶尔询问一下新项目的目标价自然无伤大雅。而对于新客户，最好还是实实在在地谈判，只有当前期工作解决、报价完成、样品确认后，仅由于价格问题一直无法推动下去，才可以向客户询问一下目标价，看看自己能否满足，为破冰做最后努力。

13 给客户推荐新产品 Recommending New Product

不管是老客户还是新客户，你都应该经常与他们保持互动，这样才不容易被对方遗忘。所以适当地跟进，保持基本的联系，是非常有必要的。当然在外贸生意场上，也比较忌讳有事没事打扰客户。毕竟大家都很忙，时间很宝贵，最好长话短说，没事尽量少骚扰对方，而推荐新产品，往往就是"没事找事"的一个很好的切入点。

New model recommendation – Portable hair dryer

To : Yamada Fujimori

Cc :

Bcc :

From : Pierre de Royer

Subject : New model recommendation – Portable hair dryer

Signature: Apple Mail!

Dear Mr. Yamada,

How are you recently？ Long time no contact with you！

Any news for the samples we sent out several months ago？ Do you have some buying plan this year？

I'd like to introduce you our new hair dryer model as below. As we guess you might be interested, we have prepared the samples beforehand. Please check the photos and instruction manual in attachment.

We have passed the testing and got the PSE certificate. Samples could be sent on request.

Thanks and best regards,
Pierre de Royer
VP- Sales & Marketing

Outline（提纲挈领）

1. Long time no contact with you！ 好久没联系!

2. buying plan：采购计划。

3. beforehand：提前，这里相当于 in advance。

4. instruction manual：说明书。

5. VP：副总裁，vice president 的简写。

More Expressions（触类旁通）

1. If it works for you, please keep me informed.
如果可行的话，麻烦您通知我。

2. It is not necessary for getting the sample at this stage. However, the price counts for much more！
这个时候没有必要看样品，更重要的是价格问题!

3. Now announcing our newest model of hair dryer.
在此（给您）推荐我们最新款的电吹风。

4. Kindly note that the EMC certification is about to expire before the end of May.
请注意，EMC 认证会在 5 月底前到期。

5. Would you like to try a small order to test the market ?

请问您是否考虑下个小单来测试市场呢？

Q&A（深入浅出）

Question :

什么是 PSE 认证?

Answer :

PSE 认证即自我合格声明，电气产品要出口日本，就必须遵循日本的《电气用品安全法》（DENAE）。它把电气产品分为强制性认证和非强制性认证两种，强制性认证的产品需要带有菱形标志的 PSE，非强制性认证的产品则需要带有圆形标志的 PSE，这都是这类产品出口到日本所必需的。

具体的 PSE 认证包括产品测试、验厂以及拿到证书后的监督。PSE 证书由日本经济产业省授权的第三方机构认证和颁发，我们常见的 SGS、BV、Intertek 之类的国际知名第三方机构，都可以对产品做此类认证。

具体要求和相关信息，可以参阅这些第三方机构的官网。

回答客户的各种问题 Replying Multiple Questions

很多时候，新客户的询盘会有一大堆的问题，回答这些问题往往是初次磨合时商谈的重要内容。因为客户对供应商完全没有了解，希望知道关于产品和公司的更多信息，这就需要业务员尽可能完整且详细地提供信息。

许多大客户和专业买家，甚至有专门格式的表格交给供应商填写，你一定要认真对待，及时处理。

Quotation details

To : May Chow

Cc :

Bcc :

From : Adeline Zhang

Subject : Quotation details

Signature: Apple Mail!

Dear May,

Thanks for getting me back for my quotation. Concerning your questions, please check our reply as follows：

1. Is it possible to do O/A 45 days？
[Adeline Zhang]： According to our company policy, we could only go ahead with T/T or L/C at sight. I think we could make a compromise to do L/C 45 days with you.

2. What is your main market？ Turnover？

[Adeline Zhang]： Our main market is the USA. And the turnover last year was 5 million USD annually, more or less.

3. Have you cooperated with other customers in Germany？ Who are they？

[Adeline Zhang]： Yes, we got orders from Otto & Lidl via importers.

4. Are you interested in doing our own designing items？

[Adeline Zhang]： Absolutely！ It's our pleasure.

5. How many staffs in your company？

[Adeline Zhang]： Almost 35 office guys and 10 inspectors.

Should you have any further questions, please feel free to contact me.

Thanks and best regards,
Adeline Zhang
Sales Manager- EU division

Outline（提纲挈领）

1. O/A：open account，也就是赊销。O/A 45 days，相当于 45 天放账，跟 T/T 45 days 几乎一致。

2. make a compromise：做出让步。

3. turnover：销售额。一般指的是全年的销售额。

4. more or less：或多或少。

5. inspector：验货员，也就是我们常说的 QC。

More Expressions（触类旁通）

1. Thanks for mailing me back.

感谢您回复我的邮件。

2. Our sales turnover last year was roughly 50 million HKD.

我们去年的销售额大约是五千万港币。

3. Have you cooperated with any customer in New Zealand？

你是否跟新西兰客户合作过？

4. It is our pleasure to be on service of you.

能为您服务，是我们的荣幸。

5. Could you please drop by our company when you're in China？

当您来中国的时候，能否抽空来一趟我们公司呢？

Q&A（深入浅出）

Question：

如果邮件写得很短，客户会不会觉得我不够专业？

Answer：

不会，事实上很多欧美客户的邮件都不会很长。因为商务人士的时间都很宝贵，工作很忙，尤其是买手、主管，每天要处理无数的工作，回复一大堆的邮件，不可能每封邮件都写很长，客套和寒暄，完全没有必要。一般都是言简意赅，几句话点明主旨，把要说、要问、要回答的事情表达清楚。熟人之间的邮件，甚至可以连抬头和署名都没有。

至于专业还是不专业，是针对产品、服务和效率而言的，跟邮件的长短没有关系。千万不能"为赋新词强说愁"，为了写邮件而写邮件，为了凑字数而加内容，为了卖弄英文而用很多长句和冷僻词，那就违背了初衷，把简单的问题复杂化，浪费对方的时间，甚至造成各种理解上的困难和误会，这才是真正的不专业！

Part 2 报价处理 Offer Methods

15 快速准确的报价 Prompt & Accurate Quotation

　　不管是对待新客户还是老客户，报价的时效性都很重要。尤其是对刚接触的潜在客户，一旦报价速度慢了，机会可能就拱手让人。

　　但是在追求效率和速度的同时，也需要注意邮件的内容和报价的质量，要快而准，不能报价后发现算错了，再去跟客户道歉，去更新报价单，这只会让客户觉得你不可靠、不专业。

Quote sheet in detail

To：Flora Gillian

Cc：

Bcc：

From：Jessica Li

Subject：Quote sheet in detail

Signature: Apple Mail!

Dear Flora,

Thanks for mailing me back and notifying us of your requested item with details.

Please check the offer sheet in detail with estimated

price in attachment. The accurate price will be fixed after sampling. I will keep you posted on this !

Your immediate reply will be appreciated.

Regards,
Jessica

Outline（提纲挈领）

1. mail somebody back ：回复某人邮件 / 信函。

2. notify ：通知，通告。

3. estimated price ：预估的价格。

4. accurate price ：准确的价格。

5. immediate reply ：快速的回复。

More Expressions（触类旁通）

1. Kindly let me know if you need any further assistance.
如果您需要任何进一步协助，请通知我。

2. You can be certain that our price is really competitive.
您可以放心，我们的价格是绝对有竞争力的。

3. Thank you for taking time to send me the inquiry.
感谢您抽出宝贵的时间来向我询价。

4. How does L/C sound ?
我们做信用证怎么样？

5. Your prompt reply will be greatly appreciated.

若您能尽快回复，我们会非常感激！

 Q&A（深入浅出）

Question：

邮件里单独的 estimate 具体指什么？

Answer：

在商务邮件里，estimate 可以做动词，也可以做名词，指"估价""大致的价格"，跟 estimated price 的含义几乎是一致的。一般要求对方报价时，可以用 offer、price、quotation、quotes，也可以用 estimate 这个单词，来表示初次询价所需要的大致价格。

沟通的初始阶段，客户往往缺乏一些准确的信息，没有确认数量，没有确认包装，没有确认细节，没有确认付款方式等，这时候的报价往往不是 final price（最终价格），而是给对方参考的 estimate（估价）。如：

1. "We ask our supplier to estimate the freight charge."（我们要求供应商估算运费。）这里的 estimate，就做动词使用。

2. "Please give me the estimate of your air compressor."（请给我你们空气压缩机的报价。）这里的 estimate，就做名词使用。

还有，detailed estimate，不是详细准确的价格，而是基于报价单里的参数和细节的报价。由于报价单会给出一些详细的信息，包括描述、材质、包装等，但依然属于估价，因为这些细节并没有得到客户的最终确认，所以不属于 final price（最终价格）。

16 详细专业的报价 Detailed & Professional Quotation

对于老客户、重要客户，或者对报价有具体要求和针对性的客户，你需要及时给出准确报价。而报价的内容，要尽可能详尽，并突出自身的优势，把能给到的信息一次性给全，最大限度避免挤牙膏式往来，节省双方时间，也在一开始就给客户树立一个专业的形象。

Pricing for grease gun

To : Clair Gross

Cc :

Bcc :

From : Kerry Hu

Subject : Pricing for grease gun

Signature: Apple Mail!

Dear Clair,

This is Kerry from ABC Trading Inc. According to your inquiry of grease gun, I was wondering if you could accept our pricing USD5.65/pc.

As per our conversation at HK Fair, the estimate USD5.35/pc was based on the neutral poly bag packaging with a barcode sticker only, not the color box as you mentioned in the previous email.

Please check our offer sheet in detail as attached. Also enclosed the instruction manual & die-cut of color box for your reference.

Your early reply will be highly appreciated.

Best regards,
Kerry Hu

Outline（提纲挈领）

1. grease gun：黄油枪。

2. neutral poly bag packaging：中性塑料袋包装（中性包装，表示包装上没有任何供应商信息或者客户信息，也没有品牌信息）。

3. barcode sticker：条形码不干胶。

4. previous email：上一封邮件。

5. die-cut of color box：彩盒设计稿的刀模图。

More Expressions（触类旁通）

1. We could provide you with a better price if the quantity raises to 10,000 pieces.
如果数量达到 1 万件，我们可以给您一个更好的价格。

2. Our subsidiary in the UK will handle the business with your company.
我们英国分公司会处理您的订单事宜。

3. The biggest problem for retail price is namely about packaging.
（影响零售价格的）最大问题就是包装。

4. Would you mind sending me some more photos about your inquired item？
能否给我多发一些您正在找的产品的图片？

5. My customer would enable me to offer the price below 5 dollars.

我客户只会允许我在5美元以内报价。

Q&A（深入浅出）

Question：

一旦价格陷入僵局，是否可以强调品质？

Answer：

价格谈判陷入僵局，是常有的事，业务员不必惊慌，也不必客户一说价格贵，就立马降价，这反而容易让客户无所适从。报价就应该是有理有据的，根据具体的描述、数量、包装等信息来核算价格，可以经得起推敲。如果客户嫌贵，是否可以考虑适当调整细节？比如说，修改包装、增加数量、改变某些配件和价格构成要素，来达到合理降价的目的。

当然，客户也有可能已经确认所有的细节，什么都不能改，但是唯一不接受的就是价格。这时业务员要有良好的心理素质，强调自身的优势，不一定是品质，也可以是稳定的出货时间、良好的服务、专业的业务团队、配合的上游供应商等，通过展现优势来取信于客户。既然你在价格上并不具备特别的优势，那就要尽量弱化这一块，想方设法引导对方去考虑自己的长处和优势，请客户综合考量。

应对客户的砍价 Discussion On Pricing Bargain

　　砍价是每个业务员都会经常碰到的事，甚至每天都要面对新老客户的砍价要求。有的客户根据产品和数量砍价，有的客户根据市场定位砍价，有的客户根据以往的采购经验砍价，还有的客户先乱砍一通，然后再通过货比三家来砍出最低价……

　　面对客户的砍价需要业务员有丰富的经验和良好的心理素质，不会被客户牵着鼻子走，更不会自乱阵脚。针对不同的客户，应该有不同的手法和应对策略。

Re: Pricing for grease gun

To : Clair Gross

Cc :

Bcc :

From : Kerry Hu

Subject : Re: Pricing for grease gun

Signature: Apple Mail!

Dear Clair,

I'm sorry we cannot accept your target price USD5.35 with color box packaging.

As I mentioned in the previous email, it based on the poly bag only. I take it for granted the 30 cents surcharge is reasonable. We could give you 15 cents off as maximum. That means, USD5.50 is our floor price.

Please help to understand our situation and back us.
Thank you !

Kind regards,

Kerry Hu

Outline（提纲挈领）

1. take it for granted：坚定地认为……

2. surcharge：额外费用。

3. 15 cents off：减少 15 美分。

4. as maximum：这里表示"这就是最大的让步"。

5. floor price：地板价，用来形容最低的价格、最好的价格。

More Expressions（触类旁通）

1. Please help to check with the buyer and give me reply soon.

请跟买手确认（价格），并尽快给我回复。

2. Would you accept EUR3.50/pc as the final price ?

您能接受每件 3.5 欧元的最终价格吗？

3. We could offer you a special discount of 10% if the quantity reaches one 40 feet full container.

如果订单数量可以达到一个 40 英尺的整柜集装箱，我们可以给您一个 10% 的特别折扣。

4. I have to re-check the price and see if we could meet your target.

我需要重新核算一下价格，看看能否达到您的目标价。

5. We are desperate to get your price approval to proceed.

我们非常需要您的价格确认，从而（把这个项目）推进下去。

 **Q&A（深入浅出）**

Question：

报价出去没有收到客户回复，多久跟进合适？

Answer：

笔者的个人意见是，不要跟得太紧。毕竟大家都很忙，客户有自己的工作要处理，未必能抽出时间，来解决你的问题或者查阅你的报价。所以一般报价过后，给对方充分的考虑和研究的时间，是有必要的。

我个人采用的原则，是 1–2–4 原则。也就是针对没回复的客户，报价后一周跟进，再两周后跟进，再四周后跟进。千万不要给客户留下一个"催命"的不好印象。虽然在谈判过程中，互动是必要的，但是要掌握好"度"，以免适得其反。

18 多轮价格谈判 Price Negotiating

初次报价之后，与客户来来回回就价格问题持续谈判，是很平常的。卖方希望维持一定的利润，买方希望拿到更好的价格，自然会出现多轮价格拉锯。这就需要谈判双方控制自己的情绪和节奏，用一定的技巧去磨合，去寻找一个能让双方妥协让步的折中点。

在这个过程中，邮件的往来务必要谨慎，不能轻易被别人试探出自己的底线。

Re: Final offer for grease gun project

To : Clair Gross

Cc :

Bcc :

From : Kerry Hu

Subject : Re: Final offer for grease gun project

Signature: Apple Mail! ⌄

Dear Clair,

To be candid with you, we have no margin to reduce the pricing again.

I understand the price is awful important to win the order, but the quality counts for much more. We couldn't debase our quality level to achieve your aim. I'm sorry.

Having discussed with top management, we decide to proceed with below suggestions：

1. USD5.50/pc, with color box packaging, based on 10,000 pcs quantity.
2. USD5.20/pc, with neutral poly bag packaging, based on 10,000 pcs quantity.
3. 3% special discount will be provided when the quantity is up to 30,000 pcs.

Please help to consider and advise which option is better for you. We realize that you have to test your local market and retail price. And we're pleased to go ahead with a trial order in a small quantity to start our business. Maybe 5,000 to 8,000 pcs is workable for you to make a decision, with no price increase.

Kind regards,
Kerry Hu

Outline（提纲挈领）

1. margin：利润。在商务英语中，大多用 margin 来替代 profit。
2. awful important：非常重要，awful 在这里做副词，相当于 very。
3. debase quality level：降低品质。
4. aim：目标。
5. top management：最高管理层。

More Expressions（触类旁通）

1. Price is important, but quality counts for much more.

价格很重要，但品质更重要。

2. It is not workable for us to place such a big order for the first time.

第一张订单我们没有办法把数量提那么高。

3. We could place a trial order to test the market.

我们可以下一个试单来测试市场。

4. Consumers could only pay for USD9.99 per piece as maximum for this item.

这个产品，消费者只会愿意在 9.99 美元单价以下考虑购买。

5. 10% discount will be provided if you double the quantity.

如果您把数量加倍，我们可以给您 10% 的折扣。

Q&A（深入浅出）

Question：

客户询价的时候不提供数量，如何报价？

Answer：

可以分梯度报价。比如，订货量为 MOQ（最小起订量）的价格是多少；为一个 20 英尺柜的数量，价格是多少；为 40 英尺柜的数量，价格又是多少……先把几个重要的点设置好，通过梯度报价，来引导不同的客户。

如果报价的时候，并没有设置好数量和梯度，业务员只是简单粗暴地报价 3 美元，那如果客户说，他要买 1 000 个，结果业务员用计算器一算，发现这单会亏损，于是立马把价格涨到 4 美元，那就会让客户非常不高兴。所以对于数量问题，如果客户没有特别注明，业务员在初次报价的时候，就要根据自己的常规订单来设置数量区间，做好梯度报价来引导客户继续谈判。

19 最终确定价格 Final Price Confirmation

多轮价格谈判后，一旦双方达成协议，就需要对价格进行最终确认。这一步完成后，才可以进展到下一步的订单操作或者产前样准备等。价格的确认是订单谈判的一个关键，必须得到客户的书面同意，拿到一个铁板钉钉的回复，这样才可以避免将来可能发生的纠纷。

Re: PI for grease gun project

To : Clair Gross

Cc :

Bcc :

From : Kerry Hu

Subject : Re: PI for grease gun project

Signature: Apple Mail!

Dear Clair,

Very glad to hear that you confirmed the price USD5.20/pc. You are no doubt aware of the neutral poly bag packaging. I'm writing today to send you the PI for running this trial order with 7,500 pcs.

Please help to check the file with unit price, packaging, carton measurement, delivery time, payment term, and so on. If no additional questions, please help to sign back this PI.

As soon as we got your final confirmation, we will do pre-production samples for your evaluation.

Best regards,

Kerry Hu

Outline（提纲挈领）

1. You are no doubt aware of：你无疑知道……

2. PI：形式发票，是 Proforma Invoice 的首字母缩写。

3. payment term：付款方式。

4. carton measurement：外箱资料。

5. pre-production samples：产前样，很多时候也会简写成 PP samples。

More Expressions（触类旁通）

1. We will arrange the production as long as we receive your email with approval.

只要收到您的确认邮件，我们就会安排生产。

2. Deal！Please send me the updated offer sheet asap.

成交！请马上把最新的报价单发给我。

3. Your final estimate is 5% higher than your competitors.

你最终的报价还是比同行高了五个点。

4. I could consider doing business with your company if 1,000 pieces workable for the first order.

如果你可以接受第一单 1 000 个的数量，我会考虑跟你们公司合作。

5. Good price ！ But we cannot accept your packaging suggestion. I will inform you of our idea later.

价格不错！但是我们没法接受你们的包装方案。我晚些时候会把我们的想法告诉你。

 Q&A（深入浅出）

Question：

客户确认价格后，我发现自己价格报错了，如何处理?

Answer：

根据笔者的经验，通常有两种处理方法：

1. 如果订单已经确认，这时候才发现问题，应当及时告知客户，你方报错价格的实情，正确的价格应该是多少，并且对于己方的失误给客户道歉。同时，也需要跟客户商量，是否双方都可以承担一点损失，将订单继续执行下去。如果客户严词拒绝，那供应商就要自己消化这部分损失，毕竟报价是自己报的，报出去的价格自然要坚持，诚信第一。

2. 如果订单还未确认，仅仅是对方认可了价格，但是并没有正式下订单过来，这时候简单跟客户说明情况，更新报价单给客户，并且对于己方的失误道歉，这也就可以了。尽管客户可能会因此不满而抱怨或者大发雷霆，但是订单只要没有确认，修改报价在生意场上是合理的。

当然，如果订单本身金额并不大，或者损失处在一个可以接受的范围内，那在一开始告知客户价格报错的同时，提出这张订单继续执行这个价格，无疑能让客户感受到供应商的"诚意"和"诚信"，这是难能可贵的，也能赢得客户的好感和尊敬，将来能争取更多的订单与合作机会。

Part 3 细节处理 Detailed Issues Follow-up

 给客户准备样品 Preparing Samples For Customers

根据国际惯例，要获得一个订单，一般需要供应商至少准备两次样品。一个是产前样，另一个是确认样。很多时候，订单生产完成或者生产中期，还需要给客户准备大货样。

这些样品都非常关键，直接影响订单的进展和双方未来的合作。所以在准备样品的环节上，供应商切不可掉以轻心！

Re: samples preparation

To : Clair Gross

Cc :

Bcc :

From : Kerry Hu

Subject : Re: samples preparation

Signature: Apple Mail! ⌄

Dear Clair,

Thank you for your email regarding the pre-productions samples and our subsequent phone conversation.

We're now doing the sampling and will send it to you next week. Please help to seal & sign back if quality approved.

Please confirm this email and that you are in agreement with its contents.

Best regards,
Kerry Hu

Outline（提纲挈领）

1. regarding：关于，相当于 concerning。

2. subsequent：后来的。

3. phone conversation：电话会议。

4. seal & sign back：封样，指的是样品签字确认，用袋子密封后快递回来，这样在最终验货时，就可以让验货员拆开封样，核对大货来检验货物品质。

5. in agreement with its contents：对内容没有异议。

More Expressions（触类旁通）

1. Samples will be ready/finished/completed in 3 days.
样品会在三天内完成。

2. We will do the finalization after receiving the samples.
我们会在收到样品后具体讨论。

3. Please do sampling as quickly as possible, as we have to show them in the

coming trade fair.

请尽快安排打样，我们打算在即将到来的展会上推出。

4. We will try our best to catch your itinerary.

我们会全力以赴，以赶上您的计划。

5. We will let you know the sampling status.

我们会告知您打样的进展情况。

⊕ Q&A（深入浅出）

Question：

产前样、确认样和大货样有什么区别？

Answer：

产前样：顾名思义是生产前给客户确认的样品，可以是确认好细节后做的样品，也可以仅仅是给客户确认品质用的类似产品。

确认样：是经过客户确认的样品，大货生产需要按照确认样来具体安排。一般情况下，做确认样的时候，要做两个以上，一个寄给客户，另一个放在公司留样。客户一旦确认，就对照手里留着的样品做大货。

大货样：是大货生产后，随机抽取，寄给客户的样品。大多数情况下，供应商在生产大货的时候，需要多做一些，一方面是验货时有些货物可能会有瑕疵，此时可以有替代品；另一方面是留一些样品在手里，将来客户返单，也容易照着做。

21 向客户询问到付账号 Requesting The Courier Account

　　一般而言，初次开展业务合作，是需要双方共同配合、共同付出的。比如卖方承担样品费，买方承担快递费，对双方就是相对公平的。除非样品的货值特别高，否则不宜向客户既收样品费又收快递费。

　　生意是相互的，大家都有付出，都有收获，这很正常。所以不用不好意思，大大方方请客户提供到付账号即可。

Re: samples preparation

To : Clair Gross

Cc :

Bcc :

From : Kerry Hu

Subject : Re: samples preparation

Signature: Apple Mail!

Hi Clair,

Samples were completed and passed our internal inspection. Please see the photos for your reference.

Could you please inform us of your courier account, if feasible ？ Or we could check with our express company for a nominal fee. I will ask Candy, my assistant, to pack them off to you.

Thanks and best regards,
Kerry Hu

Outline（提纲挈领）

1. internal inspection ：内部检验。

2. if feasible ：如果可行的话，这里跟 if possible 可以替换使用。

3. express company ：快递公司。

4. nominal fee ：实际费用。

5. pack off ：寄送。

More Expressions（触类旁通）

1. Which express company do you prefer ?
您平常用哪家快递公司？

2. The hand samples were ready.
手板样都已经完成了。

3. Please advise your account for freight collect.
麻烦您提供一下到付账号。

4. Good news ！ Pre-production samples were passed our internal inspection.
好消息！产前样已经通过了我们的内部检验。

5. We want you to look over the attached photos of samples and give us your comments.

请您看一下附件的样品图片，并提供宝贵意见。

Q&A（深入浅出）

Search

Question：

Hand sample 究竟该怎么理解？

Answer：

中文可以翻译成"手板样"。简单地说，就是在没有模具的前提下，根据客户要求做出的品质确认样。一旦客户确认，并正式下订单，供应商就可以投入资金去开模具，从而进入生产环节。

比如塑料制品，客户要求产品有一个新的造型，这个新产品是不可能凭空生产出来的，供应商需要根据情况开一套或多套模具，再通过注塑或吹塑等工艺，把塑料粒子注入模具，然后在高温下成型，做成产品。关键的问题是，模具的制作费用非常高，而且需要一个很长的周期。对于新项目，客户要看确认样，供应商往往会采取做 hand sample（手板样）的方法，等客户确认后，再谈判具体的模具费和时间等问题，把订单谈判推动到实质阶段。

22 请客户支付样品费 Requesting Sampling Charge

请客户支付样品费，一定是有选择的，不能在任何情况下都向客户收钱。比如客户的订单还没下，但是要求专门定制样品，且样品是专色或者专门的包装，甚至还有客户的商标，那供应商势必就要在打样环节投入更多的成本和费用，这就可以跟客户提出，酌情收取样品费。

Re: sample charge request

To：Clair Gross

Cc：

Bcc：

From：Kerry Hu

Subject：Re: sample charge request

Signature: Apple Mail! ⌄

Hi Clair,

Thanks for the approval for the final samples. That means, we have worked through all the points of connection.

I am writing this email for your confirmation for the film charge of USD300. And we will afford the sampling charge & freight cost. We really hope you could accept

---

this at-cost price.

Thanks in advance,

Kerry Hu

 Outline（提纲挈领）　　　　

1. points of connection：争论点，这里表示有争议的一些问题。

2. film charge：制版费。

3. afford：提供，这里指"承担"样品费和快递费。

4. freight cost：运费，这里指样品的快递费。

5. at-cost price：接近成本的价格，这里指这个制版费没有额外收取利润。

 More Expressions（触类旁通）　　　　

1. Just following up to let you know that we already did the packaging as your request.

请注意，我方已经根据您的要求做好包装了。

2. It is not necessary for the logo printing on samples at the moment.

现在不需要把我们的商标印在样品上。

3. Please do the sampling based on our 3−color logo as attached file.

请在打样的时候，参照附件的设计稿，把三色的商标做上去。

4. Enclosed please find our bank info of NZD account.

附上我公司新西兰元的银行账号。

5. We could also take credit card for sample charge.

我们可以接受信用卡支付样品费。

Q&A（深入浅出）

Question：

邮件里的 film charge 怎么理解？

Answer：

这里的 film 不是电影，而是菲林，film charge 可以理解为制版费。比如客户要求确认某个样品，但要在样品上打上客户的商标，这就涉及制版，额外的费用会随之产生，包括纸卡、彩盒等的费用。

当然，大货生产的时候，因为制版费可以分摊到每个产品上，所以无足轻重。但是做一到两个样品，就会产生几百元到几千元人民币的费用。很多时候，需要客户来承担这笔费用。

23 询问样品是否满意 Asking For Sample Evaluation

　　样品寄走后，不仅要告知客户寄样的时间，还要提供快递单号，以便客户在需要的时候查询快递进度。当然，己方也要时刻查询快递情况，看客户何时签收。一旦签收，就需要及时跟进，了解情况，如样品是否满意，哪里有缺陷，哪里需要改进，是否需要重新打样，等等，这样才能有的放矢，有针对性地将订单执行下去。

	Comments for samples	

To : Clair Gross

Cc :

Bcc :

From : Kerry Hu

Subject : Comments for samples

Signature: Apple Mail!

Dear Clair,

Have you enjoyed a nice weekend？

I'm sure you are pretty busy in Monday. I just wanna check with you the result of sample evaluation. To toot my own horn a bit, I must say the quality is really good to proceed, with bells and whistles.

I look forward to your official order soon！

Best regards,
Kerry Hu

Outline（提纲挈领）

1. pretty busy：非常忙，相当于 very busy，只是 pretty 的用法更加口语化。

2. wanna：想要，相当于 want to。

3. sample evaluation：样品评估。

4. toot my horn：自我吹嘘，王婆卖瓜，这里表示对自家的样品很有信心。

5. with bells and whistles：拥有附加值。

 More Expressions（触类旁通）

1. I am desperate to get your approval for samples.

我非常需要您对于样品的确认。

2. We look forward to receiving your confirmation in 3 days.

我们期望三天内收到您的确认。

3. There are some minor issues that I'd like to check with you.

有些小问题我想跟您确认一下。

4. I think we don't need to reinvent the wheel here.

我认为我们没有必要重复劳动。

5. We will send you one piece of sample, and keep another one on hand for record.

我们会寄给您一个样品，把另外一个留底。

 Q&A（深入浅出）

Question：

什么情况下应向客户收取样品费？

Answer：

笔者的个人意见是，可以根据不同的情况，设置三种不同的应对策略：

第一，针对老客户或重要客户，只要样品费的金额不大，完全可以由供应商承担。如果费用特别高，可以跟客户商量，比如双方分摊部分费用，共同承担开发过程中的成本。当然，这种情况下就需要特别注明，下单以后是否可以完全退还，或者未来订单金额到了多少的时候，可以逐步退还。

第二，针对新客户，可以先评估客户的情况和订单预期。如果费用在可以接受的范围内，考虑己方独自承担。如果无法负担，可以跟客户讨论由对方承担或者双方分担。

第三，针对新客户，如果样品金额相对较高，但是并没有高于快递费用，而客户又愿意承担这部分快递费，本着共同开发的商业惯例，应当由供应商承担样品费，而客户提供到付账号，或者直接支付运费。

24 讨论包装问题 Packaging Issues Discussion

即便在订单确认后，包装也是需要仔细确认的。因为寄样品一般不需要提供完整的包装，而最后在做大货的时候，则需要提供准确的最终包装设计稿，给客户确认。如果不经确认直接生产包装，一旦发现有错误，再要求改动，对买卖双方来说，都是劳民伤财的事。

Packaging issues

To：Clair Gross

Cc：

Bcc：

From：Kerry Hu

Subject：Packaging issues

Signature: Apple Mail! ⌄

Dear Clair,

Sorry to disturb you again !

According to your purchase order, the packaging is poly bag with heat transfer printing, right ？ But our previous discussion was poly bag only, without any additional charge. If you insist on going with printing, the unit price will be increased a little bit.

As an alternative, we could waive the printing charge if you could accept the sticker, instead.

Please help to check and let us know how to proceed.
Thanks.

Regards,
Kerry Hu

Outline（提纲挈领）

1. purchase order：采购合同。

2. heat transfer printing：热转印。

3. additional charge：额外费用。

4. as an alternative：另一种方案。

5. waive the printing charge：不收印刷费用。

More Expressions（触类旁通）

1. Thanks a million for your order confirmation.

万分感谢您对于订单的确认。

2. I'm particularly interested in double blister.

我特别喜欢双泡壳包装。

3. We could go ahead with the same slide card packaging like your current items.

我们可以做成插卡包装，和你们现有的产品一样。

4. What about using white box, instead？

能不能用白盒包装代替？

5. It is better to put 12 pieces in one inner box, and then 48 pieces in one outer
carton.

最好 12 件产品装一个内盒，然后 48 件产品装一个外箱。

Q&A（深入浅出）

Question：

双瓦楞纸箱如何用英文表达？

Answer：

可以简单翻译成 double corrugated carton，或者 double wall corrugated carton。

另外，单瓦楞纸箱就是 corrugated carton，三瓦楞纸箱是 triple corrugated carton，都是外贸操作中十分常见的外箱包装。一般而言，比较重的产品，或者特别易损坏的产品，就会采用多层瓦楞纸箱，避免运输过程中的撞击，保护箱子中的货物。

25　讨论颜色问题 Colors Discussion

订单操作中，颜色是很重要的一个问题。很多订单出问题，都是因为颜色跟客户的要求有偏差，严重的色差大部分客户都是没法接受的。所以实际工作中要注意，若客户指定颜色，必须让其提供专门的色号，并根据色号提供产前样或色块给客户做最终确认，确认以后才能正式安排生产。

Colors approval

To : Clair Gross

Cc :

Bcc :

From : Kerry Hu

Subject : Colors approval

Signature: Apple Mail!

Dear Clair,

Thanks for your kind notice ! Please hereby reconfirm the colors for your orders.

PMS137（orange）： 2,500 pieces
PMS362（green）： 2,500 pieces
PMS418（dark grey）： 1,500 pieces
PMS637（nattier blue）： 1,000 pieces

If no problem, we will send you some color pieces for your approval before mass production.

Best regards,
Kerry Hu

 ## Outline（提纲挈领）

1. kind notice：温馨提醒。

2. reconfirm：再次确认。

3. dark grey：深灰色。

4. nattier blue：浅蓝色，比 light blue 的程度深一点点。

5. mass production：大批量生产，这里指大货生产。

More Expressions（触类旁通）

1. Please advise the CMYK for your pattern.

请提供你们花色的 CMYK 值。

2. Please send me the color swatches for confirmation.

请提供色布给我确认。

3. Color difference is not allowed.

色差是无法接受的。

4. As you know, we have to keep the same packaging color of our items when displaying in our supermarkets.

如你所知，我方的产品在超市展示的时候，包装颜色必须保持一致。

5. We will do the final inspection strictly according to Pantone color.

最终验货的时候，我们会严格按照潘通色卡来对比颜色。

Q&A（深入浅出）

Question：

产品出现色差怎么办？

Answer：

这是现实操作中一个非常麻烦的问题，往往会直接导致客户退货甚至索赔。在实际操作中，大货生产前，必须跟客户确认好产品的颜色和对应的色卡号，并严格按照客户指定的颜色，制作确认样。只有得到客户的确认，才可以参照样品来生产大货，这个步骤绝对不能少。

现实中很多索赔，都跟色差有关。比如客户下单确认要大红色，也给了色号，但是供应商却做成了酒红色，客户能否接受？非常困难。如果客户整个系列的产品都是同一个色系，货架上别的产品都是大红色，就这批货是酒红色，他显然是无法接受的。

26 确认设计稿 Artwork Confirmation

　　订单生产之前或者生产时，需要先确认设计稿，设计稿的确认应列清楚具体细节，并请对方一一核实。一旦事后发现问题再补救，会耽误双方的时间，也会在经济上造成损失。所以在下单前或者订单操作的同时，把这些细节都确认完成，才能最大限度地把订单跟好。

Draft files for artwork

To : Clair Gross

Cc :

Bcc :

From : Kerry Hu

Subject : Draft files for artwork

Signature: Apple Mail! ⌄

Hello Clair,

Please check the files in attachment, with details below.

1. Artwork for shipping mark & side mark

2. Artwork for logo printing position

3. Draft for multi-language warnings on poly bag

4. Barcode with size

Kindly have a look and give us final approval asap.

Best regards,

Kerry Hu

 Outline（提纲挈领）

1. shipping mark：唛头。

2. side mark：侧唛。

3. logo printing position：商标印刷的位置。

4. draft：草稿。

5. multi-language warnings：多国语言警示语。

 More Expressions（触类旁通）

1. Please check the attached multi-language instruction manual.

请看附件的多国语言说明书。

2. We have to see the die-cut of color box, and then do the design.

我们需要先看到彩盒的刀模图，然后再去做设计。

3. Please send me the draft for EAN code.

请把条形码的草稿件发给我。

4. The artwork for 5-color logo will be juggled.

五色商标的设计稿需要修改。

5. I will give you the final artwork for PDQ soon.

我会把最终版本的展示盒设计稿发给你。

Q&A（深入浅出）

Question：

什么是 PDQ？

Answer：

PDQ 的来源已经很难考证，中文可以理解为"展示盒"。大部分海外朋友都认为这个词来自美国，可能最初的含义是 Pretty Damn Quick，因为使用展示盒装产品，卸货和上架时非常方便，只需拆开外箱，把整个展示盒放在货架上或者地上，消费者选择和购买产品时便可以一目了然。

关于 PDQ 的图片，大家可以通过 google 或者 bing 之类的搜索引擎，在线搜索相关图片参考。

27 了解客户的其他需求 Acknowledging Other Requests

在跟单的同时，不能闷头做事不理会客户，还需要经常与之保持互动，了解客户的其他需求，并告知客户这个订单的进展情况，时刻让客户知道，你在做事，并且进展到哪一步。"早请示，晚汇报"，在生意场上也是需要的。假设一张订单的周期是一个月，那每周一到两封邮件，跟客户保持联系，肯定是需要的。

Mass production status

To : Clair Gross

Cc :

Bcc :

From : Kerry Hu

Subject : Mass production status

Signature: Apple Mail!

Dear Clair,

How are you doing？

Regarding your current order, do you have some additional comments？

The mass production is humming alone fine. And the cartons will be completed and set up next Monday.

For the most part, it takes roughly 7 days for packing and testing. And we could carry on the final inspection

---

10 days later. Would you like to go ahead via the 3rd party？ Or just internal inspection by ourselves？

By the way, I'd like to recommend you some new items. The photos with details will send in separate emails. Please help to pay attention to your inbox.

Thanks and best regards,
Kerry Hu

Outline（提纲挈领）

1. mass production status：大货生产进展，这里的 status，也可以用 process 代替。

2. humming alone fine：进展顺利。

3. for the most part：大致说来。

4. roughly：大约，跟 about，approximately 意思接近。

5. pay attention to：留意，关注。

More Expressions（触类旁通）

1. Your order KJ–520 will be finished 15 days earlier than expectation.
您 KJ–520 的这张订单，我们会比预期提前 15 天完成。

2. My thinking is in line with you.
我的想法跟您的一致。

3. Would you like SGS to take the responsibility for the final inspection？

您想找通标标准有限公司来负责最终验货吗？

4. We found a serious problem, and would like to discuss with you on the phone. Are you free at around 2 pm this afternoon in British time？

我们发现了一个严重的问题，想跟您电话沟通。英国时间今天下午两点您方便吗？

5. Do you agree that we could redo the color box？

请问您同意我们重做彩盒吗？

 Q&A（深入浅出）

Question：

条形码用英文如何准确表达？不同国家的条形码有什么区别？

Answer：

条形码可以简单使用 barcode 来表述。而 barcode 里面，又细分为很多种，如 EAN 条形码主要在欧洲地区使用，美国则用 UPC 更多一些。中国目前的商品，也是以使用 EAN 规则的条形码为主，如今许多商品包装上又开始增加了二维码。不同国家的国别会根据编码规则在条形码上体现出来。

EAN 条形码前三位，如果在 690 到 695 之间，就表示产品在中国生产；如果是 489，就代表在中国香港生产；如果在 400 到 440 之间，就表示在德国生产。

第三天

订单操作
Orders Follow-up

Part 1　订单确认 Order Confirmation

28　收到客户订单　Receiving PO

从收到订单开始，就正式进入了"跟单"环节，因为这个时候，大部分前期的谈判已经完成，着眼点就转变成细节的处理和订单问题的跟进与再谈判。收到客户订单，是开始业务操作的第一步。

PO153-6pcs screwdriver set

To : Stephy Chen

Cc :

Bcc :

From : Eva Stevenson

Subject : PO153-6pcs screwdriver set

Signature: Apple Mail!

Stephy,

Please find the new order — PO153 — in attachment.

In a nutshell, we have hit a few snags for our domestic retail market. We need your help to change L/C at sight into T/T 30 days.

Give me the tracking number when you send out the samples.

Kind regards,
Eva

Outline（提纲挈领）

1. in a nutshell：简言之。

2. hit a few snags：碰到一些麻烦。

3. domestic retail market：国内零售市场。

4. L/C at sight：即期信用证，L/C 就是 Letter of Credit。

5. tracking number：跟踪号码，这里指的是快递单号。

More Expressions（触类旁通）

1. Attached/Enclosed you can find the order for mugs.

请看附件马克杯的订单。

2. We could only accept T/T at sight as payment term.

我们唯一可以接受的付款方式就是即期电汇。

3. Please do sampling with our confirmed Pantone number.

请根据我们指定的潘通色号打样。

4. Only a trial order will be placed at this time.

这次只会确认一个试单给你。

5. We could place a full 40 feet container if you give us 8% off.

如果能给予我们 8% 的折扣，我们可以下一个 40 英尺整柜的订单。

Q&A（深入浅出）

Question：

摔箱跌落测试（Drop Test）是什么？

Answer：

在实际订单操作中，很多客户要求做 Drop Test，这不仅是为了检验包装的品质，也是为了检验包装方式是否科学，看外箱能否保护好里面的产品。货物在运输和装卸过程中，如果箱子不够牢固，或者包装方式不够科学，很容易损坏箱子里面的货物。为了最大限度地避免损失，客户会要求在验货的时候，加上摔箱测试这个重要的环节。

因为箱子的重量不同，所以对跌落高度的要求也不同。简言之，要先确定高度，然后"一角三边六面"开始摔。一共要摔 10 次，先后顺序是先摔一个角，再摔三条边，最后摔六个面。

具体内容可以通过网络查询相关文件和测试要求。

付款方式谈判 Payment Terms Discussion

客户指定的付款方式和供应商要求的付款方式往往差异很大，这就需要通过进一步沟通来找到彼此可以接受的方案。很多时候，折中方案容易获得双方的认可，进而把谈判推动下去。

Re: PO153- 6pcs screwdriver set

To : Eva Stevenson

Cc :

Bcc :

From : Stephy Chen

Subject : Re: PO153- 6pcs screwdriver set

Signature: Apple Mail!

Dear Ms.Stevenson,

Well received your PO. Thank you !

Having checked with our sales manager, we could accept the quantity and FOB price for this order, with no increase. However, let's move on to the payment term. We cannot agree on O/A 30 days at the moment.

In our estimation, T/T at sight or L/C 30 days are operable. What is your take on the issue ?

Best regards,
Stephy

Outline（提纲挈领）

1. sales manager：销售经理。

2. with no increase：不再涨价。

3. move on to：继续（讨论）。

4. operable：可执行的，可操作的。

5. take on the issue：对此事的想法。

More Expressions（触类旁通）

1. Is it possible for you to accept L/C？ We won't settle any deposit to suppliers.
你们可以接受信用证吗？我们不会给供应商支付任何定金。

2. If you insist on doing L/C, we have no choice but to charge you 3% handling fee.
如果您坚持要做信用证，我们恐怕不得不收取 3% 的操作费。

3. It is a pity that you cannot accept our payment term. I have to transfer this order to another trading company.
很遗憾你们无法接受我们的付款方式。我不得不把订单转给另外一家贸易公司。

4. Your price is reasonable. However, the quality problem still exists.
你们（产品）的价格是合理的，可是，质量问题依然存在。

5. As per our discussion yesterday, we have to revise the PO.
如我们昨天讨论的，我们得去修改采购合同。

Q&A（深入浅出）

Question：
什么是贸易操作中的 door to door service？

Answer：

从字面上就很好理解，是"门到门服务"。很多客户比较信任供应商，或者是嫌麻烦，喜欢让供应商把货直接送到客户指定的国外仓库。这意味着供应商不仅要安排出货，还要承担海运费、保险费、到港以后的代清关、到客户仓库的内陆运费等，中间牵扯到的费用相当多，也比较复杂。

假设一个客户来自美国得克萨斯州（Texas），上海的供应商给他做 door to door service，就需要先从工厂把货运到上海港，报关、出货、海运到美国的目的港，委托当地的货运代理清关、提货，然后再把集装箱拖到客户在得克萨斯州的仓库，最后卸货，这个服务才算全部完成。

这和传统意义上的 DDU 和 DDP 条款有所不同，相当于加上了内陆部分的费用。当然，门到门也分两种，一种是代客户缴进口税，另一种是由客户自己安排缴税。

30 付款细节交涉 Negotiating Payment Issues

　　客户一般不会一次就接受供应商的要求，双方谈判经常会有多轮拉锯战，或者客户故意冷处理。这个时候，供应商就需要在坚定立场和适当让步的前提下，保持跟进，时刻关注客户态度的变化。

Payment issue for PO153

To : Eva Stevenson

Cc :

Bcc :

From : Stephy Chen

Subject : Payment issue for PO153

Signature: Apple Mail!

Hi Ms.Stevenson,

How are you getting on？

No news from you for more than 2 weeks. We sincerely hope you could understand our position for the traditional payment term to proceed.

If it is feasible, I will make the PI immediately.

Thanks and best regards,
Stephy

Outline（提纲挈领）

1. getting on：（最近）进展。

2. sincerely：真诚地，由衷地。这里是副词，放在动词 hope 之前。

3. understand our position：理解我方的立场。

4. traditional：传统的。

5. feasible：可行的，这里相当于 workable 或 available。

More Expressions（触类旁通）

1. No news from you for several days.

几天没您的消息了。

2. We have to get your further approval to proceed.

我们需要得到您的进一步确认，以便（把项目）进展下去。

3. We are friends in private, but business is business.

私底下我们是朋友，但生意归生意。

4. Well, we accept L/C 60 days finally.

好吧，我们最后同意接受 60 天远期信用证。

5. L/C 180 days ？ You killed me.

做 180 天远期信用证？您干脆杀了我吧。

Q&A（深入浅出）

Question：
美国客户邮件里提到的 HBC 是什么意思？

Answer：

HBC 在美国，通常是 Health and Beauty Care 的简写，指的是美容类产品。比如，"During my visiting to your booth at Canton Fair, I found a lot of your items matched our HBC series."（广交会的时候，我在你们摊位上发现很多适合我们美容产品系列的东西。）

最终订单确认 Confirmation For Final PO

订单生产是不能随便安排的，必须收到客户的正式确认，才能开始订单生产。否则一旦客户修改订单，一切都会前功尽弃。开始生产以后，如果需要更改，费时费力不说，也很难将损失转嫁到客户头上。

Re: Payment issue for PO153

To : Stephy Chen

Cc :

Bcc :

From : Eva Stevenson

Subject : Re: Payment issue for PO153

Signature: Apple Mail!

Hi Stephy,

I just come back from a Gift & Premium Fair in France. Regarding the payment, please do not quibble over details. Our company is reliable and honest. I suggest you do not lose sight of big picture for the long-term cooperation in the future.

I would like to say YES for this order to handle T/T at sight. Attached you could find the updated PO.

And, just call me Eva.

Best regards,
E. Stevenson

Outline（提纲挈领）

1. Gift & Premium Fair：礼品促销品展会。

2. quibble over：纠结，计较。

3. reliable and honest：诚实可信的。

4. lose sight of：忽视，忽略。

5. big picture：全局，大局。

More Expressions（触类旁通）

1. I just come back from a furniture trade show in Germany.

我刚从德国的一个家具展会回来。

2. We have one caveat on this PO.

我们对于这张订单有一个疑义。

3. D/P might be better for us.

我们更偏向于付款交单。

4. Send me PI if everything is OK.

如果没问题的话，可以发我形式发票。

5. Please give me some more time. I have to re-check it with my boss.

请多给我一点时间，我需要跟我老板再确认一下。

Q&A（深入浅出）

Question：

有了客户的 PO（Purchase Order，采购合同），是不是没必要再做 PI（Proforma Invoice，形式发票）？

Answer：

事实上，很多客户在谈判完成后下单，会提供正式的合同，也就是我们常说的 PO。这个时候供应商会核对相关内容，提出接受合同或者列出要修改的地方，然后跟客户协商。这个时候，PO 就是真正意义上的合同。但即便如此，供应商还是要尽量再做一份 PI 给客户确认，毕竟 PO 是客户做的，客户的意思有时会跟供应商的理解有偏差，若仅仅回签 PO，以后双方若对合同的条款发生争议，就比较麻烦。

PI 虽然只是形式发票，但很多客户都把它当成正式合同，双方签署的任何 PI 都是有效的。有些客户没有 PO 给供应商，只要求供应商根据确定好的产品、价格、交货期等做好 PI 给他确认，一旦确认，PI 就等同于真正的合同。

当然，还有少部分客户，仅仅把 PI 理解成一个正式的报价单，并没有当成任何跟合同有关的东西。

32 给客户形式发票 Sending Out PI

一旦收到订单并确认后，供应商需要提供一份形式发票来重新表述己方理解的内容，并等待客户确认。只要客户书面确认，就表示客户已经接受上面的内容，双方理解无误，不会出现歧义。

PI for PO153

To : Eva Stevenson

Cc :

Bcc :

From : Stephy Chen

Subject : PI for PO153

Signature: Apple Mail!

Hi Eva,

Thank you so much for the revised PO. It seems that we have got everything resolved.

Please take a gander at the PI in attachment. We need your help to chop it and sign back asap.

Any further questions, please feel free to contact me. Maybe I fell through the cracks somewhere.

Thanks and best regards,
Stephy

Outline（提纲挈领）

1. get everything resolved：把每件事情都解决了。

2. take a gander at：看一下。

3. chop：盖章，这里也可以用 stamp 作为动词，代替 chop。

4. sign back：回签。

5. fall through the cracks somewhere：有些地方有错。

More Expressions（触类旁通）

1. Kindly/Please stamp and sign back asap.

请尽快盖章回签。

2. We realize how difficult this situation must be for you.

我们理解如今的状况对您而言有多艰难。

3. Would you like to receive PI by email or by fax？

关于形式发票，您想让我发您邮件还是传真？

4. Please revise your PI and add some information below.

麻烦您修改形式发票，把下面这些内容增加进去。

5. Sorry, we have changed our company name and address as in the attached file. Please help to update it on the PI.

抱歉，我们已经修改了公司名称和地址，详情请见附件。麻烦在形式发票上更新一下。

Q&A（深入浅出）

Question：

什么是 Mail order box（邮购盒包装）？

Answer：

事实上，这是早些年就已经出现的名词。很多海外客户是做邮购的，他们直接发货给终端消费者，他们就是我们常规意义上理解的 Mail order customer（邮购商）。跟传统意义上的电视购物不同，邮购商一般都有很丰富的产品线和画册，欧美消费者通过画册挑选产品，一旦选定并购买产品，邮购商就会直接发货给消费者。这一点类似于国内的 B2C（公司对个人）的模式。因为物流途中，物品容易损坏，所以这种模式对包装的要求就特别高，专门应对摔箱测试的邮购盒包装就应运而生。

根据客户的不同要求，一般会有棕色邮购盒及白色邮购盒两种，采用 3 层或 4 层瓦楞纸来制作（如果是家具类的大件商品，瓦楞的层数要求更多），要求够结实、耐摔，里面的货物不会轻易损坏。

Part 2 产前准备 Pre-production Preparation

准备产前样 Preparing Pre-production Samples

　　根据国际惯例，正式生产前是需要先跟客户确认产前样的。确认样品后再生产，这样能最大限度地避免彼此间的误解。

Pre-production samples send out

To : Eva Stevenson

Cc :

Bcc :

From : Stephy Chen

Subject : Pre-production samples send out

Signature: Apple Mail!

Dear Eva,

I was wondering if you could look at the quality sample for us. It was the one we produced for our customer in Luxembourg, similar to your ordered item.

If quality approved, we will arrange the sampling with your ordered color and logo then. Let's get things rolling.

Have a nice day !

Best regards,
Stephy

Outline（提纲挈领）

1. I was wondering… ：我想知道……

2. look at ：检查，确认。

3. Luxembourg ：卢森堡，西欧国家。

4. similar to ：跟……类似。

5. get things rolling ：进展顺利。

More Expressions（触类旁通）

1. Please pass the sample to Mr. Jackson.

麻烦您把样品带给 Jackson 先生。

2. I have one question to raise.

我有个问题想请教。

3. The material for this screwdriver sample is CRV with rubber handle.

这个螺丝刀样品的材质是铬钒钢配橡胶手柄。

4. On the whole, the quality is good.

大体来说，品质是可以的。

5. Kindly do sampling strictly according to our Pantone code.

请严格按照我们指定的潘通色号来打样。

Q&A（深入浅出）

Question：

Pantone（潘通）色卡是什么？

Answer：

Pantone 是一家美国公司，在色彩方面是世界权威，制定了统一且流行的国际标准 Pantone 标准色卡。与普通办公室和家用传统打印机提供的 CMYK（四色印刷）不同，也有别于我们电脑上操作的 RGB（屏幕颜色）的色域，这类色卡提供了各种可供印刷和制作的颜色，在纺织、塑胶、建筑等各种材料上都被广泛应用，被称为"专色"。

如果客户有自己的颜色要求，通常供应商会请客户提供色号，比如客户说海蓝色哑光，这就很难定义。但如果客户提供了色卡号 Pantone 312U，供应商就能立刻从色卡中找到对应的颜色，制作样品的时候就可以参照色卡来调色，这样会做得比较准确。

34 下单给供应商 Placing Order To Supplier

收到客户正式订单后，确认好细节，就要尽快安排下单，以免因拖延造成生产和交货的延误。如果是贸易公司，就要马上下单给自己的上游工厂。

New order for 6pcs screwdriver set

To : Johnny Liu

Cc :

Bcc :

From : Stephy Chen

Subject : New order for 6pcs screwdriver set

Signature:　Apple Mail!

Johnny,

I got a new order from our European customer, exactly the same set as your provided sample.

It is imperative to ship the goods in 25 days. We ought to re-check the production arrangement. Customer would like to get them in Hamburg or Bremerhaven to catch their promotion season.

Please sign back the attached purchasing order.

Kind regards,
Stephy

Outline（提纲挈领）

1. imperative：紧急的，这里相当于 urgent。

2. ought to：应该。

3. Hamburg：汉堡，德国港口。

4. Bremerhaven：不来梅，德国港口。

5. promotion season：促销季。

More Expressions（触类旁通）

1. Attached is the repeat order for your review.

请看附件的返单。

2. Just the packaging should be changed this time ; others will be the same as usual.

这次仅仅需要修改包装，其他都跟以前一样。

3. Please ship the goods no later than the end of December.

请在十二月底前出货。

4. The items will be used for seasonal promotion. And you couldn't deliver them late, even one week.

这些产品将会用作季节性促销，所以你绝对不能延期出货，一个礼拜都不行。

5. No, we won't accept the shipment delay. Please deliver them by air asap.

不行，我们无法接受延期交货，请尽快安排空运。

Q&A（深入浅出）

Question：
竹纤维面料，能不能翻译成 bamboo fiber ?

Answer：

可以，但不是太专业。准确的翻译应该是 bamboo rayon。因为它本身就是一种人造纤维，单纯用 rayon 来表述更好，还能降低被目的港海关查验或测试的风险。尤其在美国，经常有竹制品被召回的案例，所以如果不是直接用竹子制成的竹制品，而是再加工产品，就要尽量少出现 bamboo 这类字眼。

35 紧急修改包装 Packaging Re-confirmation

有的时候，客户会在订单确认后，突然提出一些新的要求。比如要更改颜色，或者要更改包装之类的，让供应商紧急处理。

Packaging change-URGENT!!!

To : Stephy Chen

Cc :

Bcc :

From : Eva Stevenson

Subject : Packaging change-URGENT!!!

Signature: Apple Mail!

Stephy,

I am sorry to twist your arm.

We made some mistakes on the original artwork. Please help to check the attached file, with the updated packaging design file. Could you help to get things underway right now ?

We could pay for the extra cost, if necessary.

Best regards,
E. Stevenson

Outline（提纲挈领）

1. twist one's arm：强人所难。

2. original：原先的。

3. packaging design file：包装设计稿。

4. get things underway：着手进行。

5. if necessary：如果有必要的话。

 More Expressions（触类旁通）

1. We couldn't approve your packaging sample：too poor quality.

我们没法确认你的包装样品，质量太差了。

2. Everything is OK. Please proceed.

一切顺利，请继续下去。

3. Kindly note, we won't accept any color difference of packaging in future orders.

请注意，在未来的订单里，我们不会接受包装上的任何色差。

4. I don't think color box is a good idea. What about clamshell？

我不认为彩盒包装是一个好主意，考不考虑双泡壳？

5. Please use brown mail order box as packaging. All the cartons should pass the drop testing.

请使用棕色邮购盒包装，所有的外箱都需要通过跌落测试。

 Q&A（深入浅出）

Question：

double blister, blister card, skin card 和 slide card 有什么区别？

Answer：

double blister：双泡壳包装。

blister card：单泡壳包装。

skin card：吸卡包装。

slide card：插卡包装。

36 重新制作订单 Receiving Revised PO

请注意，细节一旦确认，一定要让客户重新传一份正式的合同。这样能最大限度地避免未来的误解和纠纷。有任何更改，都需要更新订单。

Revised purchase order-URGENT!!!

To：Stephy Chen

Cc：

Bcc：

From：Eva Stevenson

Subject：Revised purchase order-URGENT!!!

Signature: Apple Mail! ↕

Stephy,

Thank you for cutting us a break on the extra cost of packaging. We appreciate !

Please help to check the attached PO with amendment and ignore the previous one. We have settled on this packaging design for all future orders this year, without any change. Please don't worry about this.

Thanks again,
E. Stevenson

Outline（提纲挈领）

1. cut somebody a break：无私帮助，用心帮忙。

2. amendment：修改，修正。

3. ignore：忽视，忽略，这里指前面的订单作废，以这张为准。

4. settle on：决定，下定决心。

5. future orders：将来的订单。

More Expressions（触类旁通）

1. Please send me the amended PO within today.

请今天内把改好的合同发我。

2. Please check the confirmed PO in attachment, with stamp and signature.

请看附件中已经签字盖章的确认订单。

3. We found some major issues. Please see them below in red.

我们发现了几个主要问题，请看下面红色标注部分。

4. We hereby confirm this revised order. Kindly send us the hard copy.

我们在此确认这个修改过的订单，麻烦把正本寄给我们。

5. The quantity is not allowed to be changed after the order has been confirmed.

订单一经确认，数量就不能再改了。

Q&A（深入浅出）

Question：

如何用英语形容质量差?

Answer：

在邮件里，经常会用到形容品质的表述，比如 good quality 指的是质量很好。但若要表达"质量很差"，千万不能用 good 的反义词 bad，因为英文对于描述品质差有一个专门的形容词，就是 poor。

正确的说法是 poor quality。如："The cheap items are of poor quality."（这些便宜货的质量很差。）

37 重新制作形式发票 Making Revised PI

一旦客户更新订单，就要重新做好 PI 给客户确认。这是关键的一步，再烦琐也要做，既为了订单的安全，也为了避免双方的误解。标准作业流程，是一步都不能少的。

Re: Revised purchase order-URGENT!!!

To : Eva Stevenson

Cc :

Bcc :

From : Stephy Chen

Subject : Re: Revised purchase order-URGENT!!!

Signature: Apple Mail!

Dear Eva,

We're delighted to get your revised PO. Your order will be processed in one week. And we are sure the shipment plan is out of question.

Attached please find the revised PI. We need your help again to review everything and sign it back.

In the event of any discrepancies, please keep us informed.

Kind regards,
Stephy

Outline（提纲挈领）

1. delighted：高兴地。

2. process：进展，进程，这里指具体安排订单生产流程。

3. out of question：没问题。

4. in the event：如果，假如。

5. discrepancy：矛盾，不符。

More Expressions（触类旁通）

1. Here is the PI for your revised order.

这是根据您修改过的订单，做的形式发票。

2. According to my investigation, these items are currently on sale in Germany.

根据我的调查，这些产品正在德国促销。

3. Do you think it suitable for the US market？

您认为这个（方案）适合美国市场吗？

4. Absolutely not！

绝对不可以！

5. Please look it over to ensure accuracy.

请仔细检查，确保无虞。

Q&A（深入浅出）

Question：

在日常的英文邮件里，需不需要加一些关于天气之类的问候语或者别的客套话?

Answer：

英文和中文不同，写作英文和中文邮件的思维方式也有很大差异。通常来说，如果双方见面，会说一些寒暄和客套话，但若在邮件里，一般都讲究"单刀直入"。特别是近些年，邮件表达越来越口语化，"正式"的表达也开始逐渐退化，一些常用语和口语的句型和词汇，在邮件里用得越来越多。

请大家记住，对商务人士来说，时间就是金钱。效率第一，直接、简洁、点明主题即可。

38 重新准备样品 Re-arranging Samples

　　一旦客户对产品的细节做了修改，就必须重新安排样品，并请客户确认。如果仅仅是谈妥了如何修改，就贸然安排大货生产，一旦双方有理解上的差异，就会很麻烦，所以要予以重视。

Revised samples preparation

To : Eva Stevenson

Cc :

Bcc :

From : Stephy Chen

Subject : Revised samples preparation

Signature:　Apple Mail!　⌄

Dear Eva,

The samples with up-to-date color box packaging will be carried out soon. I will submit them for your approval next week, if there is no accident.

I will send you acknowledgement with tracking number then.

Best regards,
Stephy

Outline（提纲挈领）

1. up-to-date：最新的，最近的。

2. carry out：安排，完成。

3. submit：提交。

4. if there is no accident：如果没有意外的话。

5. acknowledgement：确认通知。

More Expressions（触类旁通）

1. What a relief！Please send the revised PI to me.

那我就放心了！麻烦把修改好的形式发票发给我吧。

2. Please send me the artwork in AI format.

麻烦给我发一下 AI 格式的设计稿。

3. We could accept the amendment for this PI.

我们可以接受形式发票的修改。

4. We have to negotiate the price again. It is impossible to proceed with the original price.

我们需要重新谈一下价格，用过去的价格做（这个订单）是不可能的。

5. In the meantime, the updated sample will be sent out asap.

与此同时，新的样品会尽快寄出。

Q&A（深入浅出）

Question：

邮件里常有 could you please、would you please 和 can you please 三种表达，哪种更合适？

121

Answer：

英文的表达有对应的语境，有时需要正式一点，有时需要委婉一点，有时需要突出反问的感觉，这就要具体问题具体分析。

如果单纯从礼貌和委婉的角度来看，could you please 是最委婉的，would you please 属于中等，can you please 相对来说不是太客气。如果是新客户，或者是老客户但职位级别比较高，保险起见，建议还是用 could 这个词，不太容易出错。

但是英文的遣词用句向来强调多样化，不能过多使用一个单词或者一个句型，否则会比较单调，这就需要使用者自己根据语境来把握。如果自己没有把握或者英文水平不是太高，那就建议只用 could you please，虽然不能体现英文能力，但至少不会出错。

Part 3　生产装运 Production & Delivery

39　告知客户生产情况 Advising Production Status

　　一般在货物生产过程中，业务员需要跟客户保持互动，让对方知道目前订单的进展。这样一旦有紧急情况，对方不至于措手不及。

Production status for PO153

To：Eva Stevenson

Cc：

Bcc：

From：Stephy Chen

Subject：Production status for PO153

Signature: Apple Mail!

Dear Eva,

Regarding your order PO153, the mass production is in progress and is about to be finished early next week. We'd like to get a firm answer for the inspection date, and we could get the commodities 100% finished before then.

Thanks and best regards,
Stephy

Outline（提纲挈领）

1. in progress：在进展中。

2. be about to：将要，这里跟 be going to 用法接近。

3. firm answer：确定的答复，这里是 Stephy 希望 Eva 给出一个确切的验货时间。

4. commodity：货物。

5. before then：在那之前。

More Expressions（触类旁通）

1. I think DUPRO inspection is necessary.

我认为产中验货是有必要的。

2. OK, I will send the booking to BV for final inspection according to your request.

好的，我会根据您的要求，向 BV 公司申请最终验货。

3. We will start the mass production in 7 days.

我们会在七天内安排大货生产。

4. No, any delay will be punished !

不行，任何的延迟都会被处罚！

5. We will charge you 10% if you postpone more than 2 shipments.

如果你推迟两个船期交货，我们会扣款 10%。

Q&A（深入浅出）

Question：

"整柜"和"散货"用英文怎么表达更合适？

Answer：

一般来说，整柜可以用 FCL（full container loading）来表达，散货则用 LCL（less than container loading），这是常规的叫法。比如，一个 20 英尺柜，可以写成 1 × 20' FCL，大部分客户都能看明白。

另外，也有一部分客户用 CY 和 CFS 来描述整柜和散货。这里就牵涉一个新的概念，即堆场和货运站。CY 的全称是 Container Yard，指集装箱堆场，一般在堆场里放的都是整柜出口的货物，比较方便出运，直接装船即可。CFS 的全称是 Container Freight Station，指集装箱货运站，如果是拼箱的货物，一般会放到货运站。货代会根据不同港口和出运时间，做好不同客户的货的拼箱工作。所以如果客户指出，Please ship the goods by CY，就是要求整柜出货。如果客户说，I could accept the CFS delivery，就是说他可以接受散货。

总的来说，CY 和 CFS 使用相对没有那么广泛，美国客户使用地相对较多，而其他国家和地区，还是以 FCL 和 LCL 的表达为主。

40 申请第三方验厂 Applying 3rd Party For Factory Audit

很多大客户和专业客户，在下了订单以后，一般是要进行验厂的，目的是了解供应商的真实情况，以便对未来的订单做出抉择。尤其是大单，客户对于供应商自己的工厂或上游工厂的要求是非常高的。只有第三方出具的专业报告，才能让他们对供应商有一个大致的了解。

Application for factory audit

To : Athena Zhao

Cc : Eva Stevenson

Bcc :

From : Stephy Chen

Subject : Application for factory audit

Signature: Apple Mail!

Dear Athena,

Glad to write to you！ Our esteemed customer Eva gave me your contact info.

We got their order for screwdriver set and would deliver the goods to Europe several weeks later. Now I'm writing to you for the sake of factory audit application.

It is available for us from next Monday to Wednesday.

We look forward to hearing from you soon.

Best regards,

Stephy

Outline（提纲挈领）

1. cc ：抄送，是 carbon copy 的缩写。

2. factory audit ：验厂，也经常表达为 factory evaluation。

3. esteemed ：受人尊敬的，值得尊敬的。

4. contact info ：联系方式。

5. for the sake of ：为了……

More Expressions（触类旁通）

1. The factory evaluation is compulsory.

验厂是强制性的。

2. We have to charge you USD500 as the re-audit cost, if you failed first time.

如果你第一次验厂没有通过，我们需要收取 500 美元的重验费用。

3. Please fill in the FE application file and send us back.

请填好验厂申请表，并回传我方。

4. Have you audited by other clients ?

其他客户有没有验过你们工厂？

5. We will push for the rectification which mentioned on the FE report.

我们会尽力整改验厂报告中指出的问题。

Q&A（深入浅出）

Question：

什么是 DUPRO inspection？

Answer：

DUPRO 是 during production 的简写，意为生产过程中。而 DUPRO inspection 就是指"产中验货"，当然，也可以用 inline inspection 来表达，意思是一样的。

此外，如果是货物生产完成后的最终检验，就是 final inspection。也就是说，这是最后一次的验货，验货后如果结果是通过，那就可以直接出货了。

申请第三方验货 Applying 3rd Party For Inspection

第三方验货往往是大客户和专业客户要求的，因为很多客户身在国外，国内又没有办事处之类的相关机构，这时候为了控制货物的品质和交货期，往往就会把inspection（验货）这个环节外包给第三方机构，诸如SGS, Intertek, BV, TÜV 等国际知名公司。

DUPRO and final inspection for screwdriver set

To : George Lin

Cc : Stephy Chen

Bcc :

From : Eva Stevenson

Subject : DUPRO and final inspection for screwdriver set

Signature: Apple Mail!

George,

Ask your China subsidiary to undertake one inspection case for us.

We're contemplating DUPRO & final inspection for order PO153. Kindly arrange your staffs to work on it and route the reports directly to me.

I put our supplier, Ms. Stephy Chen, in cc line. And she will contact you before long.

Regards,
E. Stevenson

Outline（提纲挈领）

1. subsidiary：分公司。

2. undertake：承接，承担。

3. contemplate：认真考虑，深思熟虑。

4. staffs：员工，是 staff 的复数。

5. route：直接发送，这里表示，Eva 要求验货公司直接把报告发给她。

More Expressions（触类旁通）

1. Our inspector will handle this case.

我们的验货员会负责这次验货。

2. The final result was NOT CONFORMED.

最终的验货结果是"没有通过"。

3. Yes, we passed the inspection according to AQL level Ⅱ.

是的，根据 AQL 等级Ⅱ的要求，我们通过了验货。

4. Be sure to route your reply directly to me.

请确保你的回复都直接发给我。

5. The final inspection and loading supervision will be handled by BV.

最终验货和监装都会由必维公司负责。

Q&A（深入浅出）

Question：

什么是验货的 AQL 标准?

Answer：

AQL 的全称是 Acceptance Quality Limit，指的是验货员在验收货物的

时候，接受的质量上限标准。因为传统的按比例抽样检验已经显得过于粗糙，不太科学，所以就慢慢发展出一套比较严谨的标准，就是我们俗称的AQL。

验货员在验货的时候，会根据 AQL 的要求核对表格，来判定合格数量和不合格数量。假设案例邮件中 Eva 向 Stephy 订购的这批螺丝总数是 3 000 套，要求是 AQL 2.5、level Ⅱ 的检验标准，那验货员核对图 3-1 所示的 AQL 表格时，就会发现 3 000 套属于"1 201 to 3 200"的区间里，对应的是"K"，然后再看下边图 3-2，K 对应的是"125"，指的就是需要抽取检验的样本数量。简单地说，就是需要抽取 125 套来检验。

Sampling Size Code Letters							
	General Inspection Levels			**Special Inspection Levels**			
Lot Size	I	Ⅱ	Ⅲ	S1	S2	S3	S4
2 to 8	A	A	B	A	A	A	A
9 to 15	A	B	C	A	A	A	A
16 to 25	B	C	D	A	A	B	B
26 to 50	C	D	E	A	B	B	C
51 to 90	C	E	F	B	B	C	C
91 to 150	D	F	G	B	B	C	D
151 to 280	E	G	H	B	C	D	E
281 to 500	F	H	J	B	C	D	E
501 to 1 200	G	J	K	C	C	E	F
1 201 to 3 200	H	K	L	C	D	E	G
3 201 to 10 000	J	L	M	C	D	F	G
10 001 to 35 000	K	M	N	C	D	F	H
35 001 to 150 000	L	N	P	D	E	G	J
150 001 to 500 000	M	P	Q	D	E	G	J
500 000 and over	N	Q	R	D	E	H	K

图 3-1

　　AQL 2.5 和 K 交集对应的"7/8"就是说，在抽样的 125 套里，查出 7 个缺陷是可以接受的，8 个就必须拒绝。在实际操作中，大家会发现，产品缺陷也是分等级的，比如 critical（严重缺陷），一般要求是 0，绝对的"零容忍"；major（重要缺陷），一般是 2.5 的标准；而 minor（轻缺陷），一般会定为 4.0。当然，根据客户和产品的不同，对于验货的要求和不同缺陷的认定也是不一样的。

Single Sampling Plans for Normal Inspection

Acceptable Quality Limits for Normal Inspection

Sample Size Code letter	Sample Size	0		0.1		0.15		0.25		0.4		0.65		1		1.5		2.5		4		6.5	
		Ac	Re	Ac	Re	Ac	Re	Ac	Re	Ac	Re	Ac	Re	Ac	Re	Ac	Re	Ac	Re	Ac	Re	Ac	Re
A	2	↓		↓		↓		↓		↓		↓		↓		↓		↓		↓		↓	
B	3	↓		↓		↓		↓		↓		↓		↓		↓		↓		↓		↓	
C	5	↓		↓		↓		↓		↓		↓		↓		↓		↓		↓		0	1
D	8	↓		↓		↓		↓		↓		↓		↓		↓		↓		0	1	1	2
E	13	↓		↓		↓		↓		↓		↓		↓		↓		0	1	1	2	2	3
F	20	↓		↓		↓		↓		↓		↓		↓		0	1	1	2	2	3	3	4
G	32	↓		↓		↓		↓		↓		↓		0	1	1	2	2	3	3	4	5	6
H	50	↓		↓		↓		↓		↓		0	1	1	2	2	3	3	4	5	6	7	8
J	80	↓		↓		↓		↓		0	1	1	2	2	3	3	4	5	6	7	8	10	11
K	125	↓		↓		↓		0	1	1	2	2	3	3	4	5	6	7	8	10	11	14	15
L	200	↓		↓		0	1	1	2	2	3	3	4	5	6	7	8	10	11	14	15	21	22
M	315	↓		0	1	1	2	2	3	3	4	5	6	7	8	10	11	14	15	21	22	↑	
N	500	0	1	1	2	2	3	3	4	5	6	7	8	10	11	14	15	21	22	↑		↑	
P	800	1	2	2	3	3	4	5	6	7	8	10	11	14	15	21	22	↑		↑		↑	
Q	1250	2	3	3	4	5	6	7	8	10	11	14	15	21	22	↑		↑		↑		↑	
R	2000	3	4	5	6	7	8	10	11	14	15	21	22	↑		↑		↑		↑		↑	

图 3-2

42 验货未通过 Failed In Inspection

第三方验货公司相对而言对货物和品质的检验会非常专业，往往能发现一些普通验货员或者工厂质检员不容易发现的问题。一旦有特别的问题，或者 AQL 超标，供应商就会被出具 Fail 或 Not Conformed 的报告，货物被拒收。还有一种情况，就是货物达到了 AQL 标准，但是还有一点小问题，验货员无法自己做主，需要和客户确认，这种情况一般就出具 Pending 或 Hold 的报告，意思是"暂定"。

Inspection failed

To : Eva Stevenson

Cc :

Bcc :

From : Stephy Chen

Subject : Inspection failed

Signature: Apple Mail!

Dear Eva,

Sorry to inform you that we failed in the final inspection. Please check the attached report from SGS, which indicated the packaging problems & surface scratches.

Due to an oversight on our part, we will arrange the re-work at once and apply for the re-inspection soon.

Sorry for the inconvenience of you.

Kind regards,
Stephy

Outline（提纲挈领）

1. SGS：通标标准技术服务有限公司，瑞士企业，国际著名的第三方测试和验货机构之一。

2. indicate：表明，指出。

3. surface scratches：表面划痕，这里用的是复数，表示有许多划痕。

4. due to an oversight on our part：由于我们的失误。

5. re-work：返工。

More Expressions（触类旁通）

1. Unfortunately, we failed in the inline inspection.

很不幸，产中验货我们没有通过。

2. We are confident we will fix all problems.

我们有信心解决所有问题。

3. We have our own inspection team to do the quality control.

我们有自己的验货团队来控制产品品质。

4. Thank you for taking the time to review the inspection report.

感谢您抽出时间来看这份验货报告。

5. No problem. We will absorb the re-inspection charge.

没问题，我们会承担重新验货的费用。

Q&A（深入浅出）

Search

Question：

在验货环节中，有时会增加 loading supervision，这是什么意思？

Answer：

Loading supervision，简单翻译就是"监装"的意思。货物完工后准备出货，需要安排集装箱装柜，这个时候是需要派业务员或者跟单员负责监装的。所谓监装，就是监视工人装柜，要确保货物被装得整齐，没有太大的缝隙，而且堆放后的货物不会在运输途中倒下，从而造成货物的损坏。

一个专业的业务员，在出货后会给客户提供监装图片，称为 loading supervision photos。主要包括集装箱的正面图片、侧面图片，打开后的空箱图片，装货 15%~20% 时的图片，装货 50% 左右的图片，装完货的图片，关半扇集装箱门能看到集装箱号等资料的图片，完全关门后的图片，箱封的图片等。

43 整改后申请重验 Applying Re-inspection

一般情况下，验货没有通过，若非得到客户的特别许可，都是需要重验的，以确保产品的质量在返工后，可以真正达到客户的要求。

Re-inspection for PO153

To : George Lin

Cc : Eva Stevenson

Bcc :

From : Stephy Chen

Subject : Re-inspection for PO153

Signature: Apple Mail!

Hi George,

Attached you can find the re-inspection booking. All the order details will be as usual, no changes for artwork and others.

We would be very anxious to proceed with re-inspection on Saturday. Please advise if this is executable for you.

And the extra cost will be totally disbursed by us. Thank you.

Best regards,
Stephy

Outline（提纲挈领）

1. re-inspection booking：重验申请。

2. as usual：跟过去一样。

3. would be very anxious to：非常渴望。

4. executable：可执行的，可实行的。

5. disburse：支付，偿付。

More Expressions（触类旁通）

1. Please see the re-inspection booking as enclosed.

请看附件的重验申请。

2. After the re-work for packaging, I'm sure we could pass the drop test this time.

我们重新做了包装，我相信这次一定可以通过跌落测试。

3. We have to do the inspection after 100% goods completed.

我们需要在货物 100% 完成后才能开始验货。

4. We are in urgent need of new color boxes as replacement.

我们急需一批新的彩盒来替换原来的。

5. Due to the quality problem, please issue the Letter of Guarantee and ship the goods accordingly.

基于质量问题，请出具保函再出货。

Q&A（深入浅出）

Question：

什么是 Letter of Guarantee（保函）？

Answer：

　　保函（Letter of Guarantee），经常简写成 L/G，是指在供应商的货不完全符合客户的要求，但问题不是太大，没有严重的质量问题，或者不会引起货物被召回的情况下，通过保证货物质量并承担相应风险的手法来按时出货。

　　供应商一旦出具保函后，就等于主动同意承担货物出运后在客户所在国的销售风险。比如包装彩盒质量比较差，供应商出具保函后按时出货，货物到客户手中后，客户发现很多产品因为包装被压坏无法销售，那客户就有权向供应商申请退货或索赔。

　　这只是其中的一种情况，现实操作中会有很多问题出现，只要不是严重的问题，而客户又急着销售这批货，往往会同意"污点放货"，但保险起见，他需要把这个风险转移到供应商身上。

44 讨论装运细节 Shipping Issues Confirmation

在生产的同时，业务员往往需要跟客户确认具体的出运方式。虽然报价时双方也许协商过一些条款，比如装运港是哪里，海运还是空运，整柜还是散货等。但在实际操作中，还可能有一些困难或者误差产生，所以在出货前，必须跟客户详细谈论出运的细节。

Shipping details for PO153

To : Eva Stevenson

Cc :

Bcc :

From : Stephy Chen

Subject : Shipping details for PO153

Signature: Apple Mail!

Dear Eva,

The goods completely passed the re-inspection by SGS. I'm so affirmative the quality for our products was substantially upgraded.

I have contacted with your forwarder, and was informed the cargo cut-off date would be next Friday.

The CBM for this order is just 19.2, not enough for a full 20' container. Would you like to ship them by LCL or FCL？

Your early reply will be appreciated.

Best regards,
Stephy

 Outline（提纲挈领）

1. affirmative：肯定的，确信的。

2. substantially upgraded：显著提高。

3. forwarder：货代。

4. cargo cut-off date：货物截关日。

5. CBM：立方米，是 cubic meter 的简写。

 More Expressions（触类旁通）

1. Kindly advise me of the cargo cut-off date.

请告诉我截关日期是几号。

2. Please ask your forwarder to re-book another quick vessel.

请让你的货代安排另一趟快船。

3. We could book 1 × 40' container, and the other goods will be shipped by LCL.

我们会订一个 40 英尺的整柜，其余部分就走散货。

4. Please accept Amsterdam as new destination port.

请接受荷兰的阿姆斯特丹作为新的目的港。

5. If you'd like us to arrange the goods by air delivery, you have to pay for the freight charge in advance.

如果您想要我们安排空运，请先支付运费。

 Q&A（深入浅出）

Question：

如果安排空运，提单复印件可否发给客户催款？

Answer：

可以，但是最好不要。因为空运和海运不同，海运提单是物权凭证，客户没有正本提单，是没有权力提货的。但是对于空运而言，没有物权凭证，只要有你的 airway bill（空运的运单）复印件，就可以从机场把货提走了。

45 告知客户出运计划 Keeping Client Informed Of ETD & ETA

一旦货物出运后，必须再次告知客户具体的航次以及预计的到港时间，好让客户了解具体情况，以便其联系目的港的货代，安排货物在当地的清关、运输及其他进口手续等。

ETD & ETA for PO153

To : Eva Stevenson

Cc :

Bcc :

From : Stephy Chen

Subject : ETD & ETA for PO153

Signature: Apple Mail!

Hi Eva,

The goods were shipped by Hyundai vessel #HY123. Please check the loading supervision report in attachment, with container number & seal number.

The sailing date was December the 27th, and the ETA might be January the 13th.

Kindly check and advise me if any further questions. Thanks.

Best regards,
Stephy

Outline（提纲挈领）

1. Hyundai vessel：韩国现代商船。

2. loading supervision report：监装报告。

3. container number：集装箱号。

4. seal number：箱封号。

5. sailing date：开船日。

More Expressions（触类旁通）

1. The goods were shipped yesterday and the ETA would be 1/25.

货物昨天已经出运了，预计到港日是 1 月 25 日。

2. It takes roughly 14 days, from Shanghai（China）to Long Beach（USA）.

从中国上海港到美国长滩港，（海运）需要 14 天左右。

3. Our warehouse is located in Connecticut. Could you provide us with door-to-door service？

我们的仓库在（美国的）康涅狄格州。你能否给我们提供门到门服务？

4. I am sure it gets off to a good start.

我确信这是一个顺利的开始。

5. The goods will be transited in Frankfurt airport and then to Oslo.

货物会在（德国）法兰克福机场中转，然后发往（挪威）奥斯陆。

Q&A（深入浅出）

Question：

什么是 cargo cut-off date, ship date, ETD 和 ETA ？

Answer ：

Cargo cut-off date ： 截关日。

Ship date ： 开船日。

ETD ： estimated time of delivery，预计出运日。

ETA ： estimated time of arrival，预计到港日。

但需要注意一点，ETD 的概念特别容易混淆。很多客户把 ETD 理解为装运时间，就是货物装入集装箱离开工厂的时间，但也有很多客户把 ETD 理解为真正意义上的"开船日"。这就造成了双方有几天甚至一周的时间差。为了避免双方的误解，笔者认为最好再补充一条 ship date，即开船日，这样比较保险。

如果从时间点的顺序来排，应该是如下的时间顺序：

先有 ETD，再有 cargo cut-off date，然后是 ship date，最后是 ETA。

第四天

收款问题
Payment Terms

46 提交单据并向客户催款
Documents Submission & Payment Push

如果订单的付款方式是即期的，出货后，需要及时提交相关单据给客户并催款，这需要第一时间来做。即使是用信用证或D/P（付款交单）之类的付款方式，单据需要提交给银行，一般也应该给客户一份单据复印件作为参考，并告知货已经出运。

○ ○ ○ Shipping documents and copy of B/L

To : Ichabod Franchi

Cc :

Bcc :

From : Liu Wei

Subject : Shipping documents and copy of B/L

Signature: Apple Mail! ◇

Dear Ichabod,

All the gazebos & hammocks you ordered were already shipped. Please check the invoice, packing list and copy of B/L in attachment.

Please help to balance the payment USD7,000 to our bank account soon.

Thanks & best regards,
Liu Wei

Outline（提纲挈领）

1. gazebo：户外露台，一般指泳池旁那种可移动的露台。

2. hammock：吊床。

3. packing list：装箱单。

4. B/L：提单，是 bill of lading 的简写。

5. to balance the payment：付清余款。

More Expressions（触类旁通）

1. Please help to settle the payment asap.

麻烦您尽快付款。

2. The goods will arrive in St. Petersburg at the end of March.

货物会在三月底到达（俄罗斯）圣彼得堡。

3. Your deposit will help a great deal for us.

你们的定金对我们非常有帮助。

4. We are fully aware of your payment policy.

我们充分理解贵公司的付款政策。

5. The order will be automatically expired if we don't receive the deposit within this week.

如果我们本周内没有收到定金，订单就会自动取消。

Q&A（深入浅出）

Question：

如何用英文准确表达"余款"？

147

Answer：

单纯表达"余款"，可以用名词 balance 或者 difference。往来商务邮件中，balance 的使用更加普遍。如：Please help to settle the balance/difference ASAP.（请尽快安排付清余款。）

当然，还可以进行意译，比如以下两个例句：

1."Tim asked whether we had arranged the rest payment."（蒂姆在问，我们是否已经付了余款。）这里，rest payment 就有"余款"的意思。

2."Please help to settle the outstanding money to our bank account."（请帮忙将余款转到我方银行账户。）这里 outstanding money 表示"未支付的钱"，同样可以理解为"余款"。

47 收到客户付款通知 Receiving Payment Advice

　　大部分客户在付款以后，都会以邮件形式通知供应商，表示款项已付，请客户寄正本提单或者安排电放等。很多时候应供应商要求，客户也会提供银行水单，用作参考，还可以在款项没有收到的情况下，提供单据让银行查询。

Payment settled

To : Liu Wei

Cc :

Bcc :

From : Ichabod Franchi

Subject : Payment settled

Signature: Apple Mail!

Hello Liu Wei,

We have transferred the difference. Please see the bank receipt in attachment.

No need to send us the original documents. Please arrange telex release for B/L.

Regards,
Ichabod

Outline（提纲挈领）

1. transfer：转账。

2. difference：余款，差额。

3. bank receipt：银行回单，也就是我们常说的"水单"。

4. original documents：正本文件，这里指正本提单，以及发票、装箱单的正本。

5. telex release：电放，指提单的电放。

More Expressions（触类旁通）

1. Please check the bank slip in attachment.

请看附件的银行回执。

2. It is not necessary for us to get the original B/L.

我们不需要正本提单。

3. Our bank informed us an error was found about your account.

我们接到银行通知，你方的银行账户有点问题。

4. Our accounting department wrongly typed your company name when transferring the payment.

我们财务部门（同事）在安排转账时，打错了你们公司的名字。

5. There is something wrong with the amount. Please re-check the invoice.

金额上貌似有点问题。麻烦您重新核对一下发票。

Q&A（深入浅出）

Question：

提单电放（Telex Release）应该如何操作？

Answer：

提单电放简言之，就是货物承运人或者代理人，回收已签发的正本提单，或者不签发正本提单，以电传形式通知卸货港，将货物交付给收货人。

它的基本流程是，供应商通知货代，提交电放申请单或者出具保函，然后货代通知船公司安排电放。原有的提单上会打上 TELEX RELEASE 或者 SURRENDERED 的字样。

但需要注意一点，提单电放的真正含义是，放弃领取提单的权利。也就是说，从电放的那一刻起，货权就不再由自己掌握，卸货港那边仅仅依靠提单复印件就可以提货。在未收到客户款项的情况下，电放提单一定要慎之又慎！

当然，电放提单的优势也是显而易见的。它可以省去国际快递耽搁的时间，操作也十分简便。特别是对于做即期 T/T 的供应商，一旦余款收到，安排电放，客户就能在目的港直接提货。

48 请客户提供银行水单 Asking Bank Receipt

　　很多时候，已经通知客户付款，但是等了多日都不见有款项到账。这个时候就需要主动询问客户，让对方帮忙查询，或者提供银行水单。因为跨境汇款的审核相当严格，收款人的账户、公司名、收款银行甚至中转行的信息都需要完全准确，任何一个细节有误，或者拼写错误，汇款都有可能被退回或者暂时冻结。

Payment issue

To : Ali Cordell

Cc :

Bcc :

From : Belinda Xie

Subject : Payment issue

Signature: Apple Mail! ⌄

Dear Ali,

Sorry to inform you we haven't received payment of the balance of USD37,544 due on our statement.

Could you please check it with your bank on a crash basis, and send us a bank slip as record？

We're sorry to trouble you and hope to receive your

---

positive reply soon.

Regards,

Belinda

Outline（提纲挈领）

1. the balance of ：余额，剩余款项。

2. due ：到期的。

3. on a crash basis ：紧急地。

4. as record ：留底，留做记录。

5. positive reply ：正面答复，这里指"好消息"。

More Expressions（触类旁通）

1. Sorry for the oversight for the balance delay.

很抱歉（我们）付余款迟了。

2. I am sure you will get the payment no later than next Friday.

我保证，你下周五之前可以收到款项。

3. The payment has been returned to your bank account.

款项已经退回到您的银行账户了。

4. Please do the wire transfer to our another bank account in Standard Chartered.

麻烦您汇款到我们另外一个渣打银行账户。

5. We have yet received the remainder of payment.

我们还没有收到余款。

Q&A（深入浅出）

Question：

收到客户发来的汇款凭证，是否可以邮寄或电放提单？

Answer：

最好不要。保险起见，还是等货款到账后再安排。因为银行的凭证未必是真实的，客户可以造假。在一些细节上故意写错信息，比如 SWIFT 号，或者公司名跟地址对应不上之类的。银行收到电汇申请后，审核发现问题，就会退回款项。

所以跨国交易要特别注意收款安全，如果款项没有到账，仅仅凭借对方的一份银行凭证，是不可以提供提单的。

49 发现付款错误跟客户重新讨论
Re-discussion For Payment Error

在收款的过程中也许会发生一些问题，比如客户付少了余款需要补上，付多了余款需要退回一部分，银行账户有问题款项被退回，或者客户把应该付给别人的钱错付给你。一旦有这类问题，都需要第一时间沟通，并拿出处理意见。

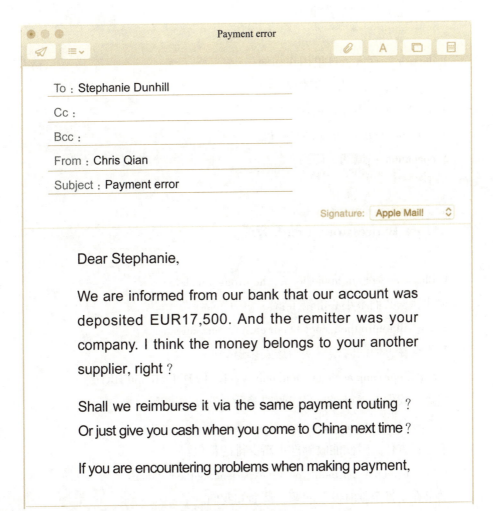

Payment error

To : Stephanie Dunhill

Cc :

Bcc :

From : Chris Qian

Subject : Payment error

Signature: Apple Mail!

Dear Stephanie,

We are informed from our bank that our account was deposited EUR17,500. And the remitter was your company. I think the money belongs to your another supplier, right？

Shall we reimburse it via the same payment routing？ Or just give you cash when you come to China next time？

If you are encountering problems when making payment,

please let us know.

Kind regards,
Chris Qian

Outline（提纲挈领）

1. deposit：存入，这里用作动词。

2. remitter：汇款人，汇款方。

3. reimburse：退款，退回。

4. same payment routing：原路径。

5. encounter：遭遇，碰到。

More Expressions（触类旁通）

1. Please accept our apologies for the wrong transfer.

请原谅，我们不小心汇错了款。

2. We will return the money at our earliest convenience.

我们会在方便的时候尽快给您安排退款。

3. Sorry, our bank account could only receive USD, EUR and HKD.

抱歉，我们的银行账户只能收取美元、欧元和港币。

4. What date can we expect to receive your re-payment？

请问我方什么时候能收到您重新安排的款项？

5. Please keep us posted if you are experiencing the balance.

如果在安排余款时发现问题，请通知我们。

Q&A（深入浅出）

Search

Question：

对于小额的样品费，怎样收款比较合适？

Answer：

小额的样品费，比如几十美元或几百美元，这时候对于客户而言电汇就不太方便了，为了这点钱跑一次银行，也是够麻烦的。另外，供应商收到的款项，同样会远远少于预期，毕竟银行的手续费也是不少的，很不合算。

所以小额支付，最好通过一些第三方平台，如 Paypal 等，相对来说费用会低廉一些。另外，Western Union（西联汇款）也是一个不错的渠道，只要提供收款人的简单信息，客户在国外也能很方便地处理，费用也不高。

50 告知客户款项收到 Payment Receiving Notification

　　收到货款后，业务员需要第一时间通知客户，并表示感谢。这不仅是基本的礼貌，也是为了节约客户的时间，不需要把精力花在跟银行确认是否电汇成功上。在平时工作中，一旦客户告知货款已经安排，业务员就应该及时查询己方的银行账户，看是否有款项入账。

Payment received with thanks

To : Sharon Doff

Cc :

Bcc :

From : Sisley Kim

Subject : Payment received with thanks

Signature: Apple Mail!

Dear Sharon,

Thanks a million for your reply enclosing the bank slip for the shipped 3 orders.The payment has been entered into our account.

Aside from this, we are immensely delighted to get your new project. Hope we could carry out broad cooperation in the near future.

Best regards,
Sisley

Outline（提纲挈领）

1. thanks a million：万分感谢。

2. enter into account：入账。

3. aside from this：除此之外。

4. immensely delighted：无比高兴。

5. broad cooperation：广泛合作。

More Expressions（触类旁通）

1. Glad to inform you that we have received your remittance.

很高兴通知您，我们已经收到贵公司的汇款。

2. I wired 5,000 pounds to your bank account.

我汇了 5,000 英镑到你的银行账户。

3. Please note that your deposit is past due.

请注意，我们还没有收到贵公司的定金。

4. Thank you for the prompt payment.

感谢您的及时付款。

5. I was wondering if you could settle HKD3,500 as deposit.

我能否请您帮忙安排 3,500 港币的定金？

Q&A（深入浅出）

Question：

跟欧洲客户做生意，是否应尽量以欧元报价结算？

Answer：

最好不要。尽管这几年人民币整体升值，美元相对走弱，但国际金融市

159

场瞬息万变，今天的强势货币，明天也许突然疲软大跌。所以即使报价前发现欧元走强，也要尽量控制风险，以免结算时遭受汇率损失。

　　笔者的个人意见是，如果不是客户的特殊要求，尽量全部以美元结算，毕竟它是国际最主要的硬通货。虽然美元近几年的预期并不是太好，但至少相对稳定，不会大起大落，可使出口企业在汇率上最大限度地避险。

51 请客户修改信用证 Proposing L/C Amendment

收到信用证，需要在第一时间审证，并通知客户具体需要修改的地方。即使供应商对条款全部接受，没有地方需要修改，也要给客户一个确认。一般情况下，客户会先提供一个草稿件，给供应商确认，然后再请银行出具正本的信用证。这样能最大限度地避免改证的费用和麻烦。

Issues to revise L/C

To : K.J. Jackson

Cc :

Bcc :

From : Alvin Sun

Subject : Issues to revise L/C

Signature: Apple Mail!

Dear Mr. Jackson,

Thank you for the L/C draft for order#DJ-199. Please find our comments in highlighted yellow below：

1. Delivery time： please extend to May 30th.
2. Payment term： please change BY ACCEPTANCE 60 DAYS FROM CARGO RECEIPT DATE into 30 DAYS, the same as our previous orders.

We wanna get your quick approval to modify the issues and open the original L/C. Thanks.

Kind regards,
Alvin Sun

Outline（提纲挈领）

1. L/C draft：信用证草稿件。

2. highlighted yellow：用荧光黄色标注。

3. extend to：推迟到……

4. by acceptance：这里指承兑信用证。

5. modify：修改，更改。

More Expressions（触类旁通）

1. Please send me the amended L/C asap.
请尽快发给我修改过的信用证。

2. We could only accept L/C at sight. 60 days is not workable for us.
我们只接受即期信用证。60 天（远期信用证）我们无法接受。

3. We hereby confirm the draft. Please help to open the original L/C.
我们在此确认草稿件，请开立正式信用证。

4. Is it possible to open L/C by HSBC or JP Morgan？
能否通过汇丰银行或者摩根大通开立信用证?

5. We would like to change the loading port to Yantian.

我们打算把装运港改成深圳盐田港。

 Q&A（深入浅出）　

Question：

表示有困难、做不到，有几种常见的邮件表达方式?

Answer：

一般来说，我们会用 difficult, almost impossible, impossible, absolutely impossible 等词汇来表示。

difficult 表示"困难、艰难"，说明事情有难度，但是并不是不能做，也不是没法做。

almost impossible 表示"几乎不可能"，这也就是说，可以试试，失败的概率很高，你要有心理准备，但也许运气很好，事情做成了也未可知。

impossible 表示"不可能"，其实已经隐含了"做不到"的意思。

absolutely impossible 是程度最重的，表示"绝对不可能"，这就是铁板钉钉的回答，意味着根本都不用尝试了，不必浪费时间。

这四种表达，程度也是由轻到重，大家在平时写邮件时，可以根据具体的情况和语境，来挑选最合适的表达。

52 请客户接受信用证不符点
Proposing Acceptance To L/C Discrepancy

信用证在交单的时候，经常会有不符点产生。在这种情况下，如果不是特别严重的问题，只要得到客户的确认，银行是可以继续偿付的。

开立信用证一般在生产前，而订单操作过程中会出现各种变数，比如客户要改一些东西，或者己方出现某某问题，但并未严重到非修改信用证不可的地步。所以，业务员就需要在交单给银行的同时，或者银行指出不符点的情况下，请客户书面确认并接受。

Please accept L/C discrepancy

To : Coco Won

Cc :

Bcc :

From : Aaron Kwok

Subject : Please accept L/C discrepancy

Signature: Apple Mail!

Dear Coco,

Sorry to get in your hair. The main thrust of this email will be the discrepancy issue of the running L/C. Please check them below which mentioned by our bank:

1. The quantity on the B/L, invoice & packing list, was not exactly the same as that in the L/C. Please forgive us for the mistake that try our best to fill entire

goods into the container, but 6 cartons were still left. We will ship them together with the next order.

2. The destination port has been changed to Rotterdam, not Hamburg.

Your colleague in shipping department was already approved the 2 issues above. I need you help to negotiate with your bank and advise them of your confirmation, to help us to get the payment soon.

Thanks and best regards,
Aaron

Outline（提纲挈领）

1. get in one's hair：打扰某人。
2. main thrust：主要内容，中心思想。
3. discrepancy issue：不符点议题。
4. entire goods：所有的货物。
5. destination port：目的港。

More Expressions（触类旁通）

1. Please allow us to deliver the goods to Vancouver directly.
请允许我们把货直接运到（加拿大）温哥华。

2. Our bank refused to accept these documents due to the discrepancy.

由于不符点的问题，我们银行拒绝接受这些单据。

3. Please send us the inspection report soon. We should submit all the documents to our bank for L/C negotiation asap.

请尽快把验货报告发给我们。我们需要尽快提交所有单据给银行议付信用证。

4. The issues above were approved by your Vice President 2 weeks ago. Please see the confirmed email in attachment.

以上这些问题，两周前你们副总已经确认接受了。请看附件的确认邮件。

5. All banking charges, including discrepancy fee and any wire commission will be deducted from the proceeds.

所有的银行费用，包括不符点费用和一切电汇的手续费，都会在付款时内扣。

Q&A（深入浅出）

Question：

用英文如何表达"辛苦你了"？

Answer：

中文跟英文的思维方式和表达习惯是有很大差异的，我们用中文进行日常对话，或者写书信电邮，经常会用到寒暄的句型，对对方的帮助表示感谢，如"辛苦你了""麻烦你了"等。

但是英文中是不能这样直译的，如果翻译成"You must be tired"，客户绝对是一头雾水，觉得很难理解。这就是文化的差异。所以我们要表达对对方辛苦帮忙的感谢，还是简单地说一句"Thank you for your kind help"或者"Sorry to trouble you"，就可以了。

53 讨论新订单付款方式 Payment Term Negotiation

很多时候，供应商对于新客户的订单会相对谨慎，特别是在付款方式方面，一般要求客户安排定金，或者以信用证的方式操作。但是时间久了，大家相互了解了，彼此生意往来都没有问题了，这个时候供应商会选择一些更加便捷的付款方式。

比如一开始合作的时候用即期信用证，慢慢就变成出运后见提单复印件付款。

Payment term for new order

To : Alexander Randolf

Cc :

Bcc :

From : Joanna Li

Subject : Payment term for new order

Signature: Apple Mail! ◇

Dear Alexander,

We have a proposal for altering the current payment term. Maybe we could go ahead with T/T or D/P at sight from the next order, in view of L/C handling charge was too expensive to our expectation.

I have talked with the top management, and they all agreed to change some flexible options for current and future orders. Please advise me of your opinion.

Thanks and best regards,

Joanna Li

Outline（提纲挈领）

1. proposal：提议，建议，提案。

2. alter：改变，修改。

3. D/P：付款交单，是英文 documents against payment 的简写。

4. in view of：由于，鉴于。

5. top management：管理层。

More Expressions（触类旁通）

1. What about doing O/A 45 days for our new order？

我们的新订单做 45 天放账怎么样？

2. L/C handling charge is expensive for trial orders.

对于试单来说，信用证的操作费太高了。

3. Please come and see us to discuss the payment terms.

请跟我们讨论一下付款方式的问题。

4. Please make payment in Australian dollars into our ABN account.

请支付澳元到我们荷兰银行的账户。

5. We will open a new SBC account. Please help to arrange the deposit later.

我们会在瑞士银行开一个新账户，请晚些时候安排一下定金。

Q&A（深入浅出）

Question：

ABN account 为什么翻译成"荷兰银行账户"？

Answer：

ABN 的全称是 Algemene Bank Nederland，在荷兰语中的意思就是"荷兰银行"。所以荷兰银行账户，可以简写为 ABN account。相应的，一些主要银行账户表达如下：

HSBC account：汇丰银行账户。

Standard Chartered account：渣打银行账户。

Citibank account：花旗银行账户。

Hang seng account：恒生银行账户。

Deutsche bank account：德意志银行账户。

SBC account：瑞士银行账户。

ANZ account：澳新银行账户。

BOC（H.K.）account：中银（香港）账户。

第五天

处理投诉
Claim Settling

54 对于品质的投诉 Quality Complaints

外贸操作中，收到投诉是经常的事，投诉内容包括品质问题、服务问题、交货期问题等，需要供应商在第一时间处理并给出答复。尤其是品质问题，往往是最重要也是最伤感情的，一旦处理不好，就会影响到双方未来的合作，必须慎之又慎。

Quality claim-IMPORTANT!!!

To : Rico Wu

Cc :

Bcc :

From : Georgio Alfred

Subject : Quality claim-IMPORTANT!!!

Signature: Apple Mail!

Rico,

We collected the cargoes which you shipped last month !

Unfortunately, almost one fourth of them were seriously damaged. I am not sure if these items were already broken before shipment.

Please check with your forwarder for further investigation. You have to pay for everything which caused my loss !

And, I would like to get the rest goods with top priority. Please ship them by air and you should bear the cost.

Regards,

Georgio

Outline（提纲挈领）

1. collect the goods：提货，取货。

2. one fourth：四分之一。

3. seriously damaged：严重损坏的。

4. further investigation：进一步调查。

5. bear the cost：承担费用。

More Expressions（触类旁通）

1. Unfortunately，20 pieces were broken terribly.

很不幸，20件货严重损坏了。

2. Please check with your factory about this claim.

请跟你的工厂讨论这个投诉问题。

3. We have no time but deliver the cargo by air immediately to catch the original schedule.

我们已经没时间了，只能立刻安排空运，去赶上原计划。

4. We still require 1/3 of the goods as replacement.

我们还需要补三分之一的货来替代。

5. Please look into this case at once！

请立刻调查这件事情的原委！

Q&A（深入浅出）

Question：

收到投诉，如何在第一时间应对？

Answer：

投诉是谁都不愿意碰到的，一旦发生，就不可避免地会造成损失。在这种情况下，供应商跟客户出于自身立场和利益的考虑，必然会有争论和不同意见。

笔者个人的处理方式是，只要收到客户的投诉，第一时间先给出正面回应，不要纠结于这是谁的错，而是先争取一定时间去思考和讨论，等公司内部达成一致的处理意见或几套处理方案后，再跟客户讨论商量。这样既有时间进行内部紧急磋商，也可以避免在客户气头上火上浇油，先冷处理一下，对双方都有好处。业务员可以这样回复客户的投诉邮件：

Dear Allen,

We got your claim message. I will do the investigation seriously and get you back asap.

Kind regards,

Ice

55 对于交货期的投诉 Delivery Time Complaints

　　交货期的投诉，是经常会有的。订单生产中有很多不稳定因素，而且客户也经常在订单操作中提出这样或那样的修改意见，这在时间上难以控制。还有货代和船公司，也有可能推迟船期，甚至有爆仓、甩柜的情况出现。这就需要业务员在收到投诉时，第一时间了解和调查清楚具体情况，给客户及时的反馈。

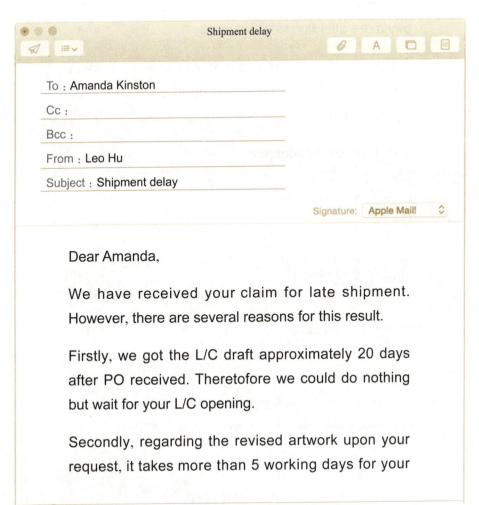

Shipment delay

To : Amanda Kinston

Cc :

Bcc :

From : Leo Hu

Subject : Shipment delay

Signature: Apple Mail!

Dear Amanda,

We have received your claim for late shipment. However, there are several reasons for this result.

Firstly, we got the L/C draft approximately 20 days after PO received. Theretofore we could do nothing but wait for your L/C opening.

Secondly, regarding the revised artwork upon your request, it takes more than 5 working days for your confirmation. And we could't do mass production prior to your approval.

Thirdly, your forwarder advised us that you already confirmed the delivery date & cargo cut-off date, and haven't doubted about the postponed shipment.

In some respects, we are also partially to blame. For instance, we should inform you some more days ago before shipment, and our merchandisers should also pay more attention to your orders.

In the near future, I'm sure that we are about to keep the communication channels open and avoid any potential danger for our business.

Thanks and best regards,
Leo

 Outline（提纲挈领）

1. theretofore：在那之前。

2. upon：根据。

3. working day：工作日。

4. prior to your approval：在您确认之前。

5. keep the communication channels open：保持沟通渠道畅通。

More Expressions（触类旁通）

1. This fault lies with our company.

这个问题是我们公司的错。

2. We are willing to accept part of the blame.

我们愿意承担部分责任。

3. There are several reasons for this delay.

交货期延误是有多种原因的。

4. I am sorry to inform you about the shipment delay on such short notice.

我很抱歉这么仓促通知您，船期需要延迟。

5. To recap, we won't accept any additional charge for this delay.

简单来说，对于这次延误我们不会承担任何额外的费用。

Q&A（深入浅出）

Question：

订单延期，是不是需要第一时间跟客户道歉？

Answer：

绝对不是！在英文交流中，sorry（抱歉）这个词是不能随便用的。当然，根据欧美国家的传统，也许大家平时都比较客气，邮件里都离不开 thank you（谢谢），appreciate（感激）之类的字眼，但是要注意，不能随便道歉。

在欧美文化中，对就是对，错就是错；一就是一，二就是二，都是直来直去的。如果这件事是你的责任，大方道歉，并提出补救方案，未尝不是一种展现诚恳态度的做法。但如果不是你的原因造成的问题，就应该据理力争，把情况说明白。尽管你依然可以帮客户想办法，帮客户补救，但是这句 sorry 是不能讲的。

很多朋友在邮件里都喜欢经常带着 sorry，对客户的询盘晚回复一天就说"sorry for late reply"（抱歉回复晚了），客户嫌价格高了就"sorry for the high

177

price, but..."（抱歉价格高了，但是……），总之，客户只要有一点不开心马上就道歉，这是要不得的！这样做会使你显得卑躬屈膝，失去做生意的双方原有的对彼此的尊重，主动把自己推到一个弱势的不利地位。

订单延期了，这很正常，先要调查和了解清楚原因，为什么延期？如何处理和解决？是谁的问题造成延期？将来如何避免和改进？这些才是应该去做和去跟客户说明的。如果己方错了，说抱歉完全应该。如果是对方的错，可以指出，并提出补救方案和建议，这反而更能得到对方的尊重和感激。

56 对于服务的投诉 Service Complaints

　　服务不够好，是做生意的大忌。靠价格取胜的时代已经过去了，中国制造的价格竞争力一直在往下走，目前就产品本身而言，依靠的仅仅是巨大的制造业潜力、熟练的工人和丰富的上下游配套供应商而已，剩下的都属于附加值范畴。所以加强服务、提高效率就变得非常有必要。专业、服务、效率，一直是被强调的外贸三要素。

Service problem apology

To : Cindy Whittaker

Cc :

Bcc :

From : Phoebe Cai

Subject : Service problem apology

Signature: Apple Mail!

Dear Ms. Whittaker,

Thank you for your email. In the first place, please accept our sincere apologies for the service defectives.

We will take full responsibility for this claim and pay for the accessory cost and express charge. I hope this unhappy incident will not let you lose the confidence to cooperate with us in future.

I already asked a third party to deal with our after-service issues in Canada and the US, and set up an 800 toll-free call. Therefore, consumers could contact this company directly for any questions when using the products. If any parts damaged, house calls will also be solved as quickly as possible.

It is our guarantee that the similar incidents will not happen again.

Best regards,
Phoebe Cai

Outline（提纲挈领）

1. in the first place：首先。

2. sincere apology：诚挚的歉意。

3. take full responsibility：负全部责任。

4. toll-free call：免费电话。

5. house call：上门服务。

More Expressions（触类旁通）

1. We will take the responsibility for this serious claim.
对于这个严重的索赔，我们会承担责任。

2. Please accept our sincere apologies！

请接受我们诚挚的道歉！

3. We will set up an 800 toll-free call for after-service.

我们将会开通一个关于售后服务的 800 免费拨打电话。

4. House calls will be solved from 9 am to 5 pm every Monday to Saturday.

我们会在周一到周六，上午九点到下午五点，上门处理问题。

5. We regret the accessories shortage caused by our omission.

由于我们的疏忽造成配件的不足，深感抱歉。

Q&A（深入浅出）

Question：

为什么要请第三方公司提供 after-service（售后服务）？

Answer：

很多产品，如电器、家具等，一般消费者购买后，是需要厂家提供相应服务的。比如买了把电锯不知道怎么用，或者买了套家具不知道怎么装，就会联系销售方或者厂方，咨询具体事宜。又或者买来的产品需要安装或者维修，这也是需要卖方提供服务的。

在欧美，商家不可能维持一个庞大的服务团队，来应付各类产品售后问题的。如果美国消费者在超市里买了一套沙发，结果回去组装的时候，发现少了几个螺丝，这种情况该怎么处理呢？一般都会直接联系超市，要求退货或者换货，然后补偿路费等损失。超市收回这套缺少螺丝的沙发后呢？这部分产品就会被退回或扣款，将损失转嫁给了供应商。这无形中就会浪费很多资源、费用、时间、成本，效率也随之降低。如果供应商不是特别大的公司，没有完善的联保体系和售后服务部门，要在各个市场维持相应的服务，就变得十分困难。

所以，在成熟的欧美市场，就出现了这一块服务的外包，即由第三方专业的服务公司来完成售后这个环节。在产品的说明书或包装上提供一个免费的售后服务电话，消费者在使用过程中遇到问题，就可以直接拨打这个电话，由专人负责处理跟进，这样，卖方就能最大限度地做好服务，把损失和成本控制在一个较低的范围。

57 道歉并提出解决方案 Apology & Solutions

　　一旦己方做错了某些事，不仅需要在第一时间向客户道歉，还需要仔细研究并给出解决方案，而不是一句简单的道歉就了事了。这对客户来说很不礼貌，也是相当不负责任的。供应商要站在客户的角度换位思考，如果这个问题发生了，客户能够怎么办？自己应该怎么做，才能尽快帮他解决困难？有什么应对的办法？

30% items will be delivered by air

To : Karina Lipson

Cc :

Bcc :

From : Lucy Yuan

Subject : 30% items will be delivered by air

Signature: Apple Mail!

Dear Karina,

This is Lucy Yuan, colleague of Katie, from ABC Trading in China. I am in charge of the sales team of EU business division.

It is our mistake to delay your orders 3 shipments than your previous schedule, due to the peak season and labor shortage before the CNY holiday. We apologize !

We totally realize that you are urgent to get the cargo for promotion and advertisement. As per my discussion with my boss, we plan to deliver 30% of goods by air, and the rest part will remain the sea transport.

Please help to check and reply me asap. And I have to call our forwarder for further arrangement. Thanks.

Kind regards,

Lucy Yuan

Sales Director

Outline（提纲挈领）

1. in charge of：负责，管理。

2. sales team：销售团队。

3. peak season：订单旺季，相对应，淡季是 off season。

4. labor shortage：劳动力紧缺。

5. sea transport：海运。

More Expressions（触类旁通）

1. I am in charge of our marketing department.

我管理我们公司的市场部门。

2. It is our mistake to postpone the delivery date to Apr.30.

把交货期推迟到四月三十日是我们的责任。

3. We could deliver them by air and pay for the freight charge.

我们会安排（货物）空运，并承担运费。

4. Please split them into 2 × 20′ containers and ship them to Bremerhaven.

请把它们分成两个 20 英尺柜出货，去德国不来梅港。

5. We will lose USD 7 000 in our estimation.

据估计，我们（这次）将会损失 7 000 美元。

Q&A（深入浅出）

Question：

在给客户的邮件里，如何表示日期？

Answer：

日期是个令人头痛的问题，即使是欧美商务人士，对于日期的表述也经常是一头雾水。比如 8/ 4/ 2012，就很难判断是 2012 年 8 月 4 日还是 4 月 8 日。如果是 13/ 4/ 2012，那就相对简单，因为月份最大就是 12，这里的 13 肯定表示 "日"，那么大家就立刻能明白它指的是 4 月 13 日。要是后面表示年份的也用简写，来个 04/ 08/ 09，那就年、月、日都分不清了。

日期的表达，大致分为 "英式" 和 "美式" 两种。

英式：日 / 月 / 年（如：8/ 7/ 19，8/ 7/ 2019 对应 8th July, 19 ；8th July, 2019）

美式：月 / 日 / 年（如：7/ 8/ 19，7/ 8/ 2019 对应 July 8th, 19 ；July 8th, 2019）

为了避免邮件往来的误会，在碰到跟日期有关的表达时，最好采用全称。如：July 8th, 2019 或 8th July, 2019。

客户提出索赔 Compensation Claim

客户提出索赔，往往都会提供具体的理由，比如货期延迟、产品质量有问题、包装破损，或者产品与客户要求不符等，这些都有可能成为客户索赔的理由。所以我们的供应商在操作订单的时候，一定要小心再小心，要控制好每个环节，细节方面多跟客户确认，可以提出建议，但不能自作主张，只有这样，才能尽可能避免索赔情况的出现。

Recall case-Top Urgent!

To : Athena Hu

Cc :

Bcc :

From : Kelly Friedman

Subject : Recall case-Top Urgent!

Signature: Apple Mail!

Ms. Hu,

We got a majority of claims of quality issue for your products. What's up？？？

The situation is vital at the moment. We have to recall all the items RIGHT NOW. The highest priority is starting recall action and doing compensation to consumers to minimize losses.

It is your responsibility to compensate everything,

which includes unit price, freight charge, import tax, retail margin, labor cost, recalling fee and any additional expense.

I will check with my accountant and make you a list soon.

Regards,
Kelly

Outline（提纲挈领）

1. vital：致命的，无比严重的。

2. highest priority：当务之急。

3. start recall action：启动召回程序。

4. minimize loss：减少损失。

5. accountant：会计师。

More Expressions（触类旁通）

1. In case of short delivery, we have no choice but to lodge a claim.
如果发现货物少装，我们将会提出索赔。

2. This compensation is voluntary, not compulsory. It is up to you to accept or not.
这笔赔偿款是自愿的，不是强制性的，你们自己决定要不要接受。

3. We feel it is fair and reasonable to ask your company to absorb this claim charge.
我方认为由贵公司承担索赔款是公平且合理的。

4. The key is to reimburse our losses.

关键问题是补偿我方的损失。

5. Continual quality problems irritated our director. We have no choice but to cancel all the orders on hand.

连续不断的质量问题让我们的领导很恼火。我们不得不取消所有手头上的订单。

Q&A（深入浅出）

Question：

如何用英文表达"增加产量"？

Answer：

供应商经常会碰到下面这种情况，当客户因为质量问题索赔时，需要紧急赶一批货出来，补给客户。这个时候根据常规情况安排生产，三十天到六十天，再加上运输的时间，显然是无法让客户接受的。因此，供应商需要迅速安排生产，并空运或另寻快船海运。

常规的用法可以直译成："We will arrange the production at once and try increasing the production quantity to ship them earlier."（我们会立刻安排生产，并千方百计提高产量，以求尽早出货。）

此外，更好的表达是用一个地道的短语 step up production，同样有"增加产量"的意思。这个句子就可以这样表述："We will step up production to ship them earlier."这样，邮件看起来明显简洁许多，更加符合商务电邮的沟通需求。

59 商量赔款金额 Compensation Negotiation

在收到客户索赔的申请后，供应商难免会面临一个严重的问题，就是赔款的数额。具体赔多少？怎么赔？有没有变通且让双方都相对容易接受的方案？这才是业务员需要考虑的。不是一味让步，或是一味强硬就可以解决问题。谈判需要技巧，需要让双方都能减少损失，为未来的合作铺平道路，而不是出了问题一味逃避责任，做一锤子买卖。

Sharing compensation charge

To : Melisa Kiv

Cc :

Bcc :

From : Louis Cha

Subject : Sharing compensation charge

Signature: Apple Mail! ⌄

Dear Melisa,

I have discussed with my boss about the compensation cost. We couldn't accept the double charge for this order.

In reality, all the items should be recalled. But it is unfair to charge us all the products cost, freight cost, import tax & your retail margin. We sent you the final samples before mass production, and were confirmed by your engineering team. It is obviously that the quality was OK.

By the way, all of our products were UL approved, and strictly according to US standard. It is unfortunately that we have to recall the products to avoid the potential danger. But in our opinion, we could realize each other to improve the situation.

Please help to find our 2 suggestions as follows：

1- We could transfer the money back for this order, without any additional charge. In future orders this year, we could keep the price and give you a 20% discount as compensation.

2- We will ship a new wave of products as quickly as possible, and accept to give you USD 3 000 as compensation cost. Please check with your manager and give me reply soon.

Best regards,

Louis Cha

Outline（提纲挈领）

1. double charge ：双倍赔偿。

2. in reality ：事实上。

3. potential danger ：潜在危险。

4. improve the situation ：改善现有的状况。

5. a new wave of products ：新的一批产品。

More Expressions（触类旁通）

1. After due consideration, we accepted to pay for GBP 800 as compensation charge.

经过相关考虑，我们同意赔付八百英镑。

2. Although we enjoy your products, we have to find an alternative because you don't have the CE certificate.

尽管我们很喜欢贵公司的产品，但我们还是得寻找其他的供应商，因为你们没有 CE 证书。

3. It is unfair to charge us all the compensation cost.

要我方承担所有的赔款是不公平的。

4. We have suffered a serious setback due to your poor quality. The claim was more than USD 3 000.

由于你方的质量问题，我们遭受了重大损失，索赔的费用要超过 3 000 美元。

5. Ship all the products back is absolutely unnecessary. Please destroy them and we will deliver a new wave asap.

把（损坏的）所有产品运回来是没有必要的。请销毁它们，我们会重新运一批新的产品过来。

Q&A（深入浅出）

Question：

如何用英文表达"销量下滑严重"？

Answer：

一般情况下，我们会用类似 bad 或者 terrible 之类的形容词，来间接表述销售情况的糟糕。比如说：

"The sales turnover last year was bad."（去年的销售总额不佳。）

"The sales figure of March was terrible."（三月的销售数据很差。）

另外还有一个单词 plummet，表示"突然下降""大幅下跌"。如："Our sales plummeted in January."（一月的销售额断崖式下跌。）

此外，跟 bottom 有关的一个词组 bottom out，可以形象表示"见底""跌到最低点"。如："Our sales dropped terribly and bottomed out in January."（我们的销售额大幅下跌，在一月跌入最低点。）

在邮件里，可以根据具体的情况和语境，灵活使用。

60 申请分批赔付 Application For Compensation Installment

客户索赔货款，是一个令人头痛的问题。如果赔了，也许这个问题解决后，后面的生意会就此终止；如果不赔，怕惹恼了客户，也会失去未来的机会。所以在认定责任后，要根据实际情况来定性，赔多少？怎么赔？这是一个很大的学问。化整为零，分批赔付，往往是一个好主意。

---

3 waves compensation

To : Floyd Black

Cc :

Bcc :

From : Mary Zhou

Subject : 3 waves compensation

Signature: Apple Mail!

Dear Floyd,

Please allow me to apologize for the wrong logo printing on the sporting bottles. While we make every effort to insure all the details are strictly according to your request, this mistake still happened. I plan to hold a meeting with our sales and order follow-up team, to improve the procedure for all the future orders and try our best to avoid any problems.

However, it is unattainable for us to accept the

compensation charge which is up to USD30,000. Because the whole order is ONLY USD9,000 !

We could make a crucial concession to pay for USD12,000 altogether, and split them into 4 orders. That means, we could refund USD3,000 this time, and accept to be deducted USD3,000 each time for the coming 3 orders.

Regarding the unusable bottles, our forwarder will deliver them from your warehouse and ship them to Russia to our other customer there, and I will send you the contact info later. We will ship a new wave of products to you within one week. Hope the alternatives could catch your schedule.

Best regards,
Mary Zhou

Outline（提纲挈领）

1. improve the procedure：改进流程。

2. unattainable：做不到的，不可能的。

3. crucial concession：极大的让步。

4. altogether：总计。

5. refund：退款。

More Expressions（触类旁通）

1. Please accept our humble apologies for these defective parts.

对于这些损坏的部件，我们深感抱歉。

2. We will split the claim charge into 4 waves.

我们会把索赔的款项分成四笔来赔付。

3. It is our crucial concession to afford the compensation charge of USD10,000.

赔付一万美元已经是我方做出的巨大让步了。

4. You guaranteed that you won't charge us any additional cost if we only ship the goods 1 shipment later.

您保证过，如果只延迟一个船期，是不会要我们承担任何额外费用的。

5. I am writing to complain the inaccurate logo printing.

我写此邮件的目的是投诉贵公司把我们的商标印错了。

Q&A（深入浅出）

Question：

如何用英文表达"百密一疏"？

Answer：

"百密一疏"这个词，英文中有一个固定搭配的句子，即 Occasionally a defective one escapes our best efforts.

如："我们尽力去避免损失，但依然百密一疏"，就可以翻译成"While we try our best to avoid any losses, occasionally a defective one escapes our best efforts."

申请延期赔付 Application For Deferred Compensation

在遇到索赔时，是不能一步就达成客户要求的，这在谈判中会把己方置于非常不利的地位。在不得罪客户的同时，也要为公司争取最大利益，减少一切损失。即便是故作姿态，也要先提出一些相应的方案，再根据情况适当做出让步，或者修改原有的计划。一旦遇到无法减免赔款金额的情况，申请延期赔付，往往能在争取时间的同时，获得客户的退让。

Compensation details

To : Eileen Longfellow

Cc :

Bcc :

From : Conrad Zhang

Subject : Compensation details

Signature: Apple Mail!

Dear Eileen,

I'm so sorry for the 20% broken of our air conditioners. As per our internal investigation, poor quality of outer cartons brought about this serious problem. We will pay close attention to our vendors and control the quality strictly from now on.

Please took 20% out when balancing the payment. And we could afford your margin loss on these items. Is it possible to settle USD10,000 as compensation？

Our big boss confirmed this amount and would settle them after 120 days. I will keep you posted on progress from this end.

Best regards,
Conrad Zhang

Outline（提纲挈领）

1. internal investigation：内部调查。

2. bring about：导致。

3. pay close attention to：密切关注。

4. from now on：从现在开始。

5. take 20% out：扣除 20%。

More Expressions（触类旁通）

1. We will keep you posted on progress from this end.
我们会持续向您汇报这边的进展情况。

2. The packaging quality didn't go our way.
包装质量并没有达到我们的要求。

3. We will make all the necessary arrangements for the replacement for defective items.
我们会做好一切必要的安排，把那些损坏的产品换掉。

4. I would like to see a cost-by-cost list of this claim.

关于这次索赔，我想要看一下具体的费用明细表。

5. Your payment is past due. Please deduct the claimed USD2,000 and settle the rest part to us ASAP.

您的付款已经延期了。请扣除索赔的两千美元，把剩余部分汇给我们。

 Q&A（深入浅出）

Question：

如何处理库存产品出货后遭遇索赔？

Answer：

要一分为二来看这个问题。

首先，要看客户是否知道这批产品是库存。如果客户知道，并确认过产品的品质，这时候可以根据当初确认的邮件和样品，向客户表达己方拒绝索赔的意见，并提供相关证据。如果客户不知道产品是库存的情况，当成新产品来采购，而品质的确是次于客户要求的，那就只能跟客户商量，部分打折，或者以补货的形式给客户补偿。最后如果双方依然谈不拢，就只能根据订立的合同来处理。

其次，要看库存产品的品质是否参差不齐，出货的产品是否跟确认的样品有很大差异。这是一定要弄清楚的。根据笔者的经验，卖库存产品往往是纠纷最多的。客户会认为，你给我的样品我能接受，但是大货的品质实在太差，我无法接受。为了避免这种情况发生，笔者往往会在库存产品中寻找品质和外观最差的几个样品，给客户确认。如果客户可以接受，那整批货出货后，遭遇索赔的概率就会大大降低。

总之，只要是销售库存产品，就要特别小心，把前期的工作做仔细，避免双方因理解的差异而造成大的误会。

62 拒绝客户赔款要求 Compensation Refusal

在遇到无理索赔时，需要据理力争，说明原因，拿出证据，而不是简单地拒绝。很多时候，客户只是以为责任是供应商的，就开始索赔。因此，只要能沟通清楚，让对方明白事情的真相和原因，一切都是可以商量的。

Compensation refusal

To：Kenji Ishiyama

Cc：

Bcc：

From：Lucas Zhu

Subject：Compensation refusal

Signature： Apple Mail! ⌄

Dear Kenji,

Your compensation request has been disallowed. It is obviously not our fault !

According to your purchase order, we should do the mass production the same as your sample. That means, we handled the OEM order for you. You already confirmed our samples and inspected all the products.

We are sorry to hear that all products should be recalled due to the patent issue in Japan. Nevertheless, you're

---

the importer for your domestic market, not us. It is your duty and obligation to do investigation and fix the problems prior to placing orders.

We profoundly hope you could realize our position.

Kind regards,

Lucas

Outline（提纲挈领）

1. disallow：拒绝，不同意。

2. patent issue：专利问题。

3. nevertheless：然而。

4. duty and obligation：责任和义务。

5. profoundly：非常地，相当地。

More Expressions（触类旁通）

1. It is your work to check the patent issue, not us.

确认是否存在专利问题是你们要去做的，而不是我们。

2. It is not our responsibility for the poor packaging. Everything was approved before production.

包装质量差不是我们的责任。一切都在生产前得到（贵公司的）确认。

3. Sorry to hear that all the items should be destroyed.

很抱歉获悉，所有的产品都需要销毁。

4. Your claim expense list is not clear enough. We won't pay for this charge.

您的费用清单不够清楚详细，我们不会付这笔钱。

5. You have left us no choice but to take legal action.

你们让我方别无选择，只能诉诸法律。

Q&A（深入浅出）

Question：

拒绝客户索赔的邮件，需要循序渐进，还是开门见山？

Answer：

根据中国人的习惯，说明一件事情往往先列举原因，然后层层递进，最后摆明态度。但是英文正好相反，需要开门见山，一开始就表示接受或者拒绝，然后再说明理由。

很多朋友一收到客户的索赔邮件，第一句话就是道歉，然后写一大堆解释的话，最后再表示拒绝。在西方人的思维里，对就是对，错就是错，对就不需要承担责任，错就应该承担相应后果。一开始说了 sorry，就让对方本能地觉得你方是错了，并且已经承认了错误。即便后面有相应的解释，也会让对方觉得你是在推卸责任，会适得其反。

所以英文邮件的行文，需要开门见山。如果不是己方的责任，你方不会接受客户的索赔，那在第一句话或者第一段就直接拒绝。后面再把原因简洁清楚地表达出来，这样会更容易解决问题。

63 讨论其他方式代替赔款 Compensation Alternatives

索赔不一定都需要用钱来解决。很多客户索赔，目的是弥补他的损失，但如果能用别的办法弥补他的损失，何不灵活变通一下，跟客户谈谈呢？不到万不得已，是不能轻易赔款的。

只要有得谈，就要尽一切努力避免赔款。可以用一些别的办法，比如下次合作时给客户打个折，遇到损坏的产品时给客户重新补一批货，或者发一些别的产品过去，免费让客户试销。总之具体问题具体分析，就能找出谈判的切入点。

Compensation alternatives

To : Edward Collins

Cc :

Bcc :

From : Nancy Chen

Subject : Compensation alternatives

Signature: Apple Mail!

Dear Edward,

We would like to express our deeply regret that the barcode for 10% goods couldn't be scanned. It is too expensive to do the re-work in EU.

Hence, we will ship you another 10% goods by air as replacement. Is it acceptable to give us 20 days？

If time limited, we suggest you try our new model KJ-295. We have stock for this item, and the quality is better than your ordered KJ-294. These products could be delivered in 3 days after packaging.

Please give us your feedback. Thanks.

Kind regards,
Nancy

Outline（提纲挈领）

1. express our deeply regret：表达我们深深地遗憾。

2. barcode：条形码。

3. hence：因此。

4. time limited：时间有限，这里表示时间不允许。

5. stock：库存。

More Expressions（触类旁通）

1. We would like to express our deeply regret that the goods couldn't be shipped on time.

对于货物不能准时出运这件事，我们深表歉意。

2. If time limited, we could deliver them by air.

如果时间不够，我们可以安排空运（货物）。

3. We have this microwave oven in stock.

这款微波炉我们还有存货。

4. The labor cost for re-work is too expensive in the UK.

在英国，（产品）返工的人工成本太高了。

5. Due to the quantity shortage of 8%, what about a 12% discount in next order ?

由于这一单出运的产品数量少了 8%，我们下一单给您 12% 的折扣怎么样？

 Q&A（深入浅出）

Question :

如果产品出口到国外后，发现包装上的条形码扫不出来，是否需要重新寄一批条形码不干胶给客户替代？

Answer :

理论上是可以的，但是采用这种方法忽略了一个重要的问题，就是治标不治本。条形码不干胶收到后怎么办？需要安排工人去一个一个检查，一个一个贴，这中间的费用和人工成本也是要考虑在内的。而且这些费用都是需要供应商承担的。所以在提供解决方案之前，要先仔细衡量和计算一下，哪种方案是最经济且损失最小的。是退货回来重新返工再出口？还是寄一批条形码过去，让客户安排返工，己方承担所有费用？抑或发一批新的产品来替代？又或者让第三方公司来负责这些返工事宜？

这些都需要跟客户讨论，找到双方都能接受的折中方案。如果不商量就直接给客户寄一批条形码不干胶过去，是不负责任的表现。

第六天

售后跟进
After-sale Service

64 询问产品销售情况 Inquiring Sales Condition

外贸产品销售以后，是需要保持跟进，了解进展的。比如产品在当地市场的销售情况如何？消费者有什么反馈？有哪些地方需要改进？跟市场上同类产品相比有什么优缺点？价格上是不是有足够的竞争力？这些都是需要跟客户讨论的，对业务员未来的订单操作会很有帮助。

Updated purchasing plan

To : Annie Lo

Cc :

Bcc :

From : Sky Zheng

Subject : Updated purchasing plan

Signature: Apple Mail!

Hi Annie,

Long time no see !

I would like to check with you about the distribution and retail status. Is everything OK ？ Anything else we can do for you ？

We haven't got your orders since 6 months ago. Do you have updated purchasing plan or programs ？

Kind regards,
Sky

Outline（提纲挈领）

1. long time no see：好久不见。

2. distribution：分销。

3. retail status：零售情况。

4. since 6 months ago：从六个月前到现在，这种表达一般用于完成时态。

5. updated purchasing plan：新的采购计划。

More Expressions（触类旁通）

1. We haven't received your orders since 3 months.

我们已经三个月没有接到您的订单了。

2. What about the current status for Belgium market？

现在比利时市场的情况如何？

3. Could you advise your purchasing plan this year？

能否告诉我们贵公司今年的采购计划？

4. Metro gave us a big order for this item. I would like to check if you have the interest.

关于这款产品，麦德龙下了一个大单给我们。我想了解一下，你们公司是否也有兴趣。

5. If we act quickly, we could sell the items in Canada before June.

如果动作够快，我们可以让这些产品6月前在加拿大销售。

Q&A（深入浅出）

Question：

如何用英文准确表达"时间不够"？

Answer：

我曾经看到一种错误的表达：The time is not enough. 这是完全直译的中式英语，是错误的。在英文中，可以根据上下文的语境做出合适的翻译，常规的表达大致有以下几种：

1. "There isn't enough time."

2. "The time is limited."

3. "We are running out of time."

65 了解最新市场动向 Realizing Up-to-date Market Trend

供应商要时刻关注市场信息，了解最新情况，并根据海外市场的变化，来判断和制订销售方案。对供应商而言，闭门造车不可取，这会使你跟外部环境脱节。要了解市场、了解需求、了解消费者偏好，才能有的放矢，有针对性地跟潜在客户谈判，赢得订单和机会。

Silicone cover set for mobile device

To : Jill Green

Cc :

Bcc :

From : Steve Liu

Subject : Silicone cover set for mobile device

Signature: Apple Mail!

Dear Jill,

Please allow me to introduce our new line of product, silicon cover set for mobile device.They are designed and produced for iPhone & iPad.As I know, these accessories have done well in US market. Would you like to evaluate the samples at the moment？ I'm sure it is good for promotion or general merchandise.

Do you have some idea for the hot-selling models in auto and DIY field？ I'm going to the US next week, not only for attending the Las Vegas fair, but for visiting TARGET, HOME DEPOT, and WALMART to find some interesting items as well.

I sincerely hope to see you then to discuss for our future projects. I have interest to develop some new products for US & Canadian market.

Yours faithfully,
Steve Liu

Outline（提纲挈领）

1. new line of product：新产品线。

2. have done well：卖得不错。

3. promotion：促销。

4. general merchandise：常规销售。

5. not only..., but... as well：不仅……而且……

More Expressions（触类旁通）

1. This refrigerator had done well in Italy last year.

这款冰箱去年在意大利卖得不错。

2. We produced a mini mobile charger for all series of iPhone.

我们为全系列的苹果手机开发了一款迷你充电器。

3. You are going to love our newest design！

你一定会喜欢我们最新的设计！

4. We decide to establish a sales representative office in Melbourne.

我们决定在（澳大利亚）墨尔本市建立一个销售代表处。

5. We have to do promotion every week to attract more consumers.

我们需要每周都进行促销，以吸引更多消费者。

Q&A（深入浅出）

Question：

如何理解 general merchandise ？

Answer：

这是跟一些 seasonal（季节性）的产品相对应的。大买家和专业客户，采购都是非常有计划的，每一季的产品，不同节日的产品，都是一一对应的，会一个项目一个项目地做。

而 general merchandise，通常指的是常规产品，日常销售，没有太明显的季节性。比如说，马克杯，一年四季都要销售，也都可以销售，不管促销与否，这就属于 general merchandise。

通俗一点说，就是季节性产品，供应商是不可以延期交货的，否则错过了销售季，或许就要等明年，又或许客户不再有需要。但是 general merchandise，哪怕你延期三个月，还是有办法重新制订销售计划，重新上架。

66 讨论同类产品 Similar Products Discussion

　　业务员不仅要了解自己的产品，也需要了解同行的类似产品，以及别的客户正在销售的产品。一个产品能被消费者认可，必然有其成功的道理，供应商需要根据市场情况总结和思考，找到适合自己的定位。价格是一个影响产品竞争力的因素，但如何让产品差异化更需要供应商认真研究。

Improved cordless drill by Li-ion battery

To：Gail Kipper

Cc：

Bcc：

From：Wendy Q

Subject：Improved cordless drill by Li-ion battery

Signature: Apple Mail!

Dear Gail,

I am sending you a file of a product spec in PDF version. It is our improved cordless drill which powered by Li-ion battery. The quality and working time is far better than our current model.

As far as I know, lots of US retailers begin to use Li-ion power tools. I hope it could satisfy you with just 15% price increase than the Ni-MH one. And the suggested retail price in US is $49.99.

Please ask FedEx to pick up a sample from our office.
Thanks.

Best regards,
Wendy Q

Outline（提纲挈领）

1. cordless drill ：无线电钻。

2. Li-ion battery ：锂电池。

3. Ni-MH battery ：镍氢电池。

4. as far as I know ：据我所知。

5. suggested retail price ：建议零售价。

More Expressions（触类旁通）

1. We adored this sample.
我们非常喜欢这次的样品。

2. Though the quality is far better, we couldn't accept the price increase.
尽管（这次的新产品）质量上好了很多，但是我们无法接受涨价。

3. I have to make sure if our competitor could provide the exactly same item with 20% discount.
我需要确认我们的同行是否能提供一样的产品，但价格低 20%。

4. What about the retail price for this item in Hong Kong ?
这个产品在香港的零售价是多少?

5. It is our most valuable travel charger with low price.

这是我们性价比最高的旅行充电器。

Q&A（深入浅出）

Question：

英文邮件的称呼后面是否全部用逗号？

Answer：

这是英文跟中文的差别，中文的书信，都是在称呼后面跟冒号，然后另起一段写正文。英文则不然，称呼后都是紧跟逗号的。不论前面加的是 Dear, Hi 还是 Hello，后面跟名字，又或者直呼其名，都用逗号作为标点符号隔开。

只有一种情况例外，当不知道对方收件人是谁，或者写给对方公司任何一个看邮件的人，以"敬启者"作为称呼，英文是"To Whom It May Concern"，后面是需要接冒号的。如下面这封邮件案例：

To whom it may concern：

This is Nicole from ABC Trading, LLC. It has come to my attention that your company is involved in the retail of ceramic plates.

Could you please advise the contact info for your purchasing department？ I could send you our quotes accordingly.

Best regards,
Nicole

针对缺陷提供改进方案 Solutions To Defectives

　　产品有缺陷是正常的，一个产品从最初研发，到被消费者和市场认可，需要一个过程，中间会经历很多次的修改。这就需要业务员跟客户保持互动，根据己方的理解来优化产品，给客户改进方案以供他选择。

Packaging amelioration

To : Marie Thompson

Cc :

Bcc :

From : Maggie Li

Subject : Packaging amelioration

Signature: Apple Mail!

Dear Marie,

I suggest we change the outer carton into 3-layer corrugated carton. The ones in last order were just 2-layer items, and were easily broken when delivery.

You are running the mail-order business, and the solid packaging is really important. Each carton should pass the drop test, to make sure the boxes are strong enough to protect the goods inside.

The unit price has to be added USD 0.40/pc. Let's go

50 and 50, OK？

Kind regards,

Maggie Li

Outline（提纲挈领）

1. packaging amelioration：包装改进。

2. corrugated carton：瓦楞纸箱。

3. solid：结实的。

4. drop test：外箱跌落测试，也被简称为摔箱测试。

5. go 50 and 50：一人一半。

More Expressions（触类旁通）

1. Let's go half and half.

咱们就一人承担一半吧。

2. I am sure that you will agree that improving the packaging is reasonable.

我相信您会同意，改进包装很合理。

3. I think there is still some room for improvement.

我认为（这个产品）依然有改进空间。

4. I'm thinking of building a new tooling for replacement.

我在考虑做一套新的模具来替代。

5. What about using heat transfer printing instead of silk printing？

为什么不用热转印来代替丝网印刷？

Q&A（深入浅出）

Question：

邮件和口语中，一人承担一半，如何用英文表达？

Answer：

英文中经常会碰到这类用法，涨价的时候一人承担一半，索赔的时候一人承担一半，产品出问题的时候一人承担一半，这个"一半"是难免的。准确的英文表达大致有以下几种：

【口语化】"Let's go 50 and 50."

【书面化】"50% cost should be paid by your side."

【正式的】"We suggest that we share the cost by half and half."

【非正式】"You 50%, me 50%."

业务员需要根据具体的语境，联系上下文，选择合适的表达方式。

68 对于降低成本的建议 Cost Reduction Advice

一旦谈判由于价格谈不拢陷入瓶颈，一个重要的解决方式就是修改产品的部件或包装，想办法节省成本，降低价格，以达到客户的期望或目标。如果客户觉得价格高，供应商在做出不严重影响产品品质的改进后，应即时通知客户具体修改的地方和能够节约的成本，供其参考和做出选择。

Suggestions to reduce the unit price

To : Dan Clamp

Cc :

Bcc :

From : Dylan Dong

Subject : Suggestions to reduce the unit price

Signature: Apple Mail! ↕

Dear Dan,

It is really difficult to meet your target price for USD0.90/pc. We checked several times, and found it impracticable to make it below 1 dollar.

The only suggestion is to change the TPR material into PVC, to reduce the cost. The pricing would be better, but the item couldn't pass the Phthalates testing according to EU regulations. What is your target market？ Europe or Middle East？

Please advise me of some more information to go ahead. Thanks.

Kind regards,
Dylan

Outline（提纲挈领）

1. impracticable：做不到的。

2. TPR：热塑性橡胶材料，是 Thermo-plastic-rubber 的简写。

3. PVC：聚氯乙烯，是 Polyvinyl chloride 的简写。

4. phthalates：邻苯二甲酸盐，是 phthalate 的复数，有多种相关的化学物质，多用于增塑剂。

5. Middle East：中东。

More Expressions（触类旁通）

1. What about doing it smaller to control the cost ?

能不能（把产品）做小一点来控制成本？

2. JPY3,500 is out of our target. Please reduce the cost and make the price to JPY2,200 finally.

3,500 日元超过了我们的目标。请降低费用并把价格做到 2,200 日元。

3. The price is in line with our price range, if the quality is the same as your other items.

如果质量跟你们其他产品一样的话，这个价格我们可以考虑。

4. Please double your order quantity to reduce the cost.

请把订单数量加倍从而降低成本。

5. We are willing to go down the price if you could pay for the tooling cost.

如果你方支付模具费，我们愿意把产品的价格降下来。

 Q&A（深入浅出）

Question：

如何回复客户的索赔？

Answer：

一般有三种方式：一是接受，二是拒绝，三是拖延。根据不同的场景，可以大致用以下句型回复客户：

1. 直接接受型

"I am sorry for the defectives. We will afford all the claim charge."

对于产品的品质问题我非常抱歉，我方会承担所有赔款。

2. 委婉拒绝型

"To be honest, it is not our mistake to cause the claim. Please check the issues in detail as below."

坦白说，不是我们的问题造成损失，请看以下的具体内容。

3. 暂时拖延型

"Sorry to hear that the claim issue happened. We will do the internal investigation, and give you reply soon."

很抱歉听到索赔的事情发生。我们会做内部调查，并尽快给您答复。

笔者个人的意见是，不要在第一时间就过于爽快地答应客户的全部要求。不管己方有足够理由，还是毫无道理，都需要有一个迂回的时间作为缓冲，为接下去的谈判营造一些有利的条件，所以笔者更加倾向于第三种方式。

69 给客户专业的意见 Professional Advice

外贸谈判中，要时刻体现自身的"专业性"。客户在询价或者寻找相关产品的时候，业务员要根据自己的经验和对目标市场的了解，给出有建设性的建议，让对方避免损失，少走弯路，降低成本，减少不必要的麻烦。

Testing issue and suggestions for German market

To : Alice Hawk

Cc :

Bcc :

From : Daniel Wang

Subject : Testing issue and suggestions for German market

Signature: Apple Mail!

Dear Alice,

Thank you very much for the inquiry for melamine bowls.

Please help to find the quotes in attachment. I have to inform you that these models are not suitable for German market, because of the very strict testing issues. We have to ask a 3rd party to do the testing not only for Non-PAHS, Non-Phthalate and EN71, but for LFGB as well. And the material couldn't be related to REACH SVHC list.

So my opinion is using PP or ABS, instead. We could purchase the food grade raw material, and be sure that we could pass the testing easily.

I could provide you with the quotes based on PP or ABS in another email. Would you like to check the samples in melamine, PP and ABS？

Thanks and best regards,
Daniel Wang

Outline（提纲挈领）

1. melamine：密胺树脂，它还有一个大家熟知的"可怕"名字，三聚氰胺。

2. PAHS：多环芳烃，是 Polycyclic Aromatic Hydrocarbons 的简写，因为对人体有害，所以是欧美重点监控的化学物质。

3. LFGB：是德国食品级检测。凡是跟食物接触的产品，包括围裙，在德国市场销售，都必须达到 LFGB 的要求。

4. PP：聚丙烯，是 Polypropylene 的简写，塑料的一种。

5. ABS：一种合成塑料，是 Acrylonitrile Butadiene Styrene 的简写。

More Expressions（触类旁通）

1. We will consider switching to a better supplier.
我们会考虑换一个更好的供应商。

2. We sincerely urge you to consider our offer with different material.
我们强烈要求您考虑一下另外一种材料的报价。

3. Please allow me to illustrate the functions for our multi-functional hand tool kit.

请允许我介绍一下这个多功能工具套装的功用。

4. Would you like us to print the multi-language warning on the polybag ?

请问您想要我们在塑料袋上印刷多国语言警示吗？

5. This is to inform you that your new design is not workable.

写这封邮件的目的是告诉您，你们的新设计是不可行的。

Q&A（深入浅出）

Question：

什么是 REACH ？ SVHC List 又是什么？

Answer：

事实上，REACH 的全称是 Regulation on Registration, Evaluation, Authorization and Restriction of Chemicals，是欧盟对于化学品的注册、评估、许可和限制。

这是欧盟为了加强对产品材料的控制提出的法令，比原来的 RoHS 的指令范围更广、涉及面更全，几乎涵盖了所有出口到欧盟的产品。根据现有的 REACH 指令，供应商需要注册产品中涉及的每一种化学成分，并根据欧盟的要求区分安全性。

而 REACH 涉及的材料列表又分为两大块，第一块是 Restrict Substance List（限用物质列表），第二块是 SVHC List（通报物质列表）。如果产品使用的材料属于限用物质列表，往往会被禁止使用及在欧盟销售，如重金属镉（Cd）、全氟辛烷磺酸（PFOS）、偶氮染料（AZO Dye）等。如果产品涉及通报物质列表，就需要经许可才能允许使用。

这对于供应商是非常严格的要求，不仅强调材料的环保无毒，还强调产品的安全和对环境的保护。很多客户，为了避免潜在风险，甚至连 SVHC List 上列明的所有物质，也是一律禁止使用的。所以要开发欧盟市场，掌握和了解 REACH 法规是相当有必要的。

具体细节可参阅欧盟官方网页，搜索跟 REACH 有关的内容：https：//ec.europa.eu/info/index_en.

70 推荐其他同系列的产品 Other Series Recommendation

一旦跟客户就某一产品或某一项目进行接触，业务员要适当地推荐自己销售情况不错的类似产品，或与其相关的某个系列的产品，这是争取合作机会的一个很好方式。假设客户询问了一款灯的价格，那很显然他对灯具类产品有兴趣，那推荐性价比高的、新的，或者特别低价的其他类似款，就有机会赢得新的询价。

New dining sets and swing chairs

To：Pierre Losbichler

Cc：

Bcc：

From：Ronnie Xu

Subject：New dining sets and swing chairs

Signature: Apple Mail!

Dear Mr. Losbichler,

My name is Ronnie. We met at the Tendence Fair in Frankfurt last year. At that time, you informed us that you were sourcing for one supplier for willow furniture set. Our quote sheet and samples were sent to you before the CNY holiday. Do you have some comments on our samples or pricing？

Recently, we developed some new dining set and swing

chairs for EU market. Please find the quotes with photos in attachment.

We plan to attend the Ambiente Fair next week. Hope to see you then.

Regards,
Ronnie Xu

Outline（提纲挈领）

1. source：寻找（货源、供应商）。
2. CNY holiday：中国春节假期。
3. willow furniture set：编藤家具组套。
4. dining set：餐桌餐椅组套。
5. swing chair：摇椅。

More Expressions（触类旁通）

1. Let me tell you more about our auto products.
让我再给您介绍一下我们的汽配产品。

2. I have attached a file containing photos, descriptions & packing measurement.
我已经附上文档，包含图片、产品描述和包装信息。

3. What's going on with the samples evaluation？
样品测试得怎么样了？

4. I will look into it and get back to you.
我会查一下再给您答复。

5. It would be my pleasure to do the presentation for our new product for 2020 spring.

能（由我来）给您做 2020 年春季的新产品介绍是我的荣幸。

Q&A（深入浅出）

Question：

Tendence Fair 和 Ambiente Fair 分别指什么？

Answer：

Tendence Fair 是德国法兰克福秋季消费品博览会，一般每年 8 月举行；而 Ambiente Fair 是相对应的法兰克福春季消费品博览会，一般每年 2 月举行。

这两个展会在国际上都是重量级的，对于开发欧洲市场十分重要，消费品、礼品、杂货类产品都非常适合参与这两个展会。展会上每年都聚集了大量的欧洲进口商和零售商，以及世界各地的参展商和专业买手，在行业性展会里有着举足轻重的地位。详见官方网址：

"http：//tendence.messefrankfurt.com/frankfurt/en.html."

"http：//ambiente.messefrankfurt.com/frankfurt/en.html."

71 **给客户最新产品信息** Latest Products Information

　　若产品更新换代，或者新产品上市，需要第一时间通知老客户，以便其有充足时间来开发市场，或者及时调整市场策略。一旦你的信息延迟或滞后，让客户没有及时做好准备，让新产品冲击了他的本土市场，而他原有的库存压力又较大，这都容易让他在资金和销售上出现问题，处于被动的境地。

CRV screwdriver bits kit

To : Sam White

Cc :

Bcc :

From : Tony Yu

Subject : CRV screwdriver bits kit

Signature: Apple Mail!

Dear Sam,

Sorry to trouble you at the moment. I would like to check with you about your last order for 56 pcs CRV screwdriver bits kit. Have you sold them out?

Now we developed a similar set which used carbon steel, instead. The pricing could be roughly 30% lower. We plan to roll out a promotion in the Netherlands this June. Do you have interest in this set?

Samples could be provided on request. Thanks.

Kind regards,

Tony

Outline（提纲挈领）

1. screwdriver bits kit：钻头组套。

2. sell out：卖完。

3. carbon steel：碳钢，金属的一种。

4. roll out：铺开，全面进行。

5. the Netherlands：荷兰。

More Expressions（触类旁通）

1. I want to check to make sure all of our products were sold out.

我想确认一下我们的产品都已经被卖完。

2. I wish you would reconsider trying our new and improved item.

但愿您能重新考虑一下我们更新换代的产品。

3. What sort of artwork file do you require？

（你们可以）用什么样的文件设计稿？

4. Please place an order before next weekend due to the price raise of raw material.

由于原材料价格上涨，请下周末之前确认订单。

5. We are willing to give a 2% discount if you could confirm the improved item.

如果您能确认改进过的产品，我们愿意给您 2% 的折扣。

Q&A（深入浅出）

Question：

邮件的结尾，如果要表示感谢，除了简单的 thank you，还有别的写法吗？

Answer：

表示感谢的词句，在英文书信中会经常碰到，邮件是冷冰冰的，不如面对面交谈这么自然，遣词用句的好坏往往会影响阅读者的心情，从而在主观上影响对方的判断。所以用词需要谨慎，不能出言不逊，也不能给人狂妄自大的感觉。

除了 thank 这个词外，还有 appreciate，它在程度上更深一点，也可以用 be grateful for（doing）sth. 这个词组。大致可以用以下几种表达方式。

【正式用法】"I would appreciate your assistance."

【非正式用法】"Appreciated."

【正式用法】"I'm grateful for your help."

【非正式用法】"Greatly grateful！"

【正式用法】"Could you please give me a helping hand？"

【非正式用法】"Could you help me out？"

72 告知售后服务电话 After-sale Service Hotline

　　大宗商品或者电器、医药等专业性较强的产品，是需要有专门的售后服务电话为消费者答疑解惑的。同时，售后服务也需要处理一些销售过程中的损坏和赔偿问题。这个电话号码，一般标注在产品包装上比较醒目的地方，或者在产品说明书上明确标识。如果客户没有要求，或者遗忘，业务员应当主动告知。

Toll-free hotline

To : Joey Turner

Cc :

Bcc :

From : Ross K.

Subject : Toll-free hotline

Signature: Apple Mail!

Dear Joey,

Regarding our electric shaver, we will put our toll-free hotline 800-×××-××× on both the color box and the instruction manual.

A consulting company in France does the after-sale service for us, for call answering, accessories replacing, etc. We plan to establish our own overseas office in Benelux and Sweden, and will do it by ourselves in the near future.

We think it could generate cost savings & great efficiency to boost customer satisfaction.

Best regards,
Ross

Outline（提纲挈领）

1. electric shaver：电动剃须刀。

2. consulting company：咨询公司。

3. Benelux：比荷卢，是 Belgium（比利时）、Netherlands（荷兰）和 Luxembourg（卢森堡）的统称。

4. generate：产生，创造。

5. boost：增加，促进，提升。

More Expressions（触类旁通）

1. We will establish our subsidiary for product designing in Norway next year.
我们明年会在挪威开一个子公司，专门负责产品设计。

2. This company does after-sale service for us.
这家公司帮我们处理售后服务事宜。

3. Please call the toll-free hotline if any questions.
有任何问题可以打我们的免费服务热线。

4. The telephone number for after-sale service department will be printed on the packaging.
售后服务电话会印在包装上。

5. If you need any further assistance, please contact with us.

如果您需要任何进一步的协助，请与我们联系。

Q&A（深入浅出）

Question：

电邮往来能否使用缩写？

Answer：

这要看实际情况，如果是非常熟悉的客户，一般为了节省时间，可以用一些双方都经常使用的单词或短语缩写。如聊天工具中使用的一些快捷短语，也可以适当在电邮往来中使用。

但若是新客户、不熟悉的客户，或者对方是级别较高的主管或老板，还是尽量用全拼，避免使用简写和缩写，以免让人觉得你不专业或不正式。当然，pls（please），ASAP（as soon as possible），inc（incorporated），ltd（limited）等常用缩写还是没问题的。

另外，cu2nite（see you tonight），f2f（face to face）这类短语，在电邮中经常使用就显得有些不合适了。语境和场合都很重要，当然，为了避免不愉快的事情发生，全部用正式的书写方式而不用缩写，是肯定没问题的！

第七天

其他日常工作
Other Daily Working

73 出差的自动回复 Auto-reply For Business Trip

出差期间，往往不能在第一时间处理邮件，如果身在国外，甚至有可能两三天才会看一下邮箱。为了避免让客户久等，或者错过某些重要事项，需要在邮箱里设置好自动回复。让客户知道，有紧急的事情，如何联系到你，或者应该联系谁。

Cindy's absence from 14 Jul. to 1 Aug.

To : To whom it may concern

Cc :

Bcc :

From : Cindy Tsui

Subject : Cindy's absence from 14 Jul. to 1 Aug.

Signature: Apple Mail!

Dear Sir or Madam,

I'm not in the office from 14 Jul. to 1 Aug., and have limited time to reply emails in that period.

For any urgent issues, please contact my colleague Ms. Jenny Chow at +852-xxxx-xxxx, or jennychow@xxx.com.

Sorry for the inconvenience.

Best regards,
Cindy Tsui

Outline（提纲挈领）

1. to whom it may concern：敬启者。

2. not in the office：不在公司，这里指在休假或者是其他原因没上班。

3. limited time：有限的时间，这里表示很少有时间。

4. in that period：在那段时间里。

5. urgent issue：紧急事件。

More Expressions（触类旁通）

1. Please contact with me directly as Tom is on annual leave these days.

因为汤姆最近在休年假，（有事）请直接与我联系。

2. I have limited time to check emails recently.

近来我不太有时间查收电邮。

3. Please call my mobile for any top urgent issues.

任何十万火急的事情，麻烦您直接打我手机。

4. I will be back on May 12th.

我会在 5 月 12 日回公司。

5. I have to reschedule my next trip to Osaka.

我需要重新安排我接下来去大阪的行程。

Q&A（深入浅出）

Question：

自动回复是否需要分类?

Answer：

从实际操作上来说，是需要的。专业的业务员会在出差或休假前，把自动回复邮件写好两份，保存起来。一份是 internal（内部的），另一份是 external（外部的）。前者发给公司的同事，后者发给公司以外的人。邮件的侧重点可以有所不同。

前者可以告诉同事，自己什么时候什么原因不在公司，有重要问题可以联系谁，有其他问题可以联系谁。而外部邮件通常都比较正式，只涉及业务方面的问题，应固定几个联系人负责公司的对外联系，这样不会让客户感觉很混乱。

74 通知客户展会安排 Fair Arrangement Inform

　　供应商一旦决定参加某个展会，应该在第一时间通知现有和潜在的所有客户，争取与其见面的机会。尤其是一些大的综合性展会和国内外的行业展，都有可能与现有客户或潜在客户见面，寻找新的合作机会。一般情况下，需要在半个月前就通知客户，然后三天前再提醒一次，以免客户遗忘或者没有找到相关邮件。

Canton Fair booth number

To : Leslie Miller

Cc :

Bcc :

From : Lily Wu

Subject : Canton Fair booth number

Signature: Apple Mail!

Dear Leslie,

Glad to inform you that we will attend the Canton Fair Phase Ⅱ & Phase Ⅲ this fall. Please find our booth number below：
Phase Ⅱ：11.1A16-17
Phase Ⅲ：10.3A11

Have you got a free minute then？ We could sit down face to face, and discuss the seasonal products for

2019. I am full of confidence that the items will be your best bet.

Hope to meet you and Alec by then.

Best regards,
Lily Wu

Outline（提纲挈领）

1. Canton Fair Phase Ⅱ & Phase Ⅲ：广交会二期和三期。

2. fall：秋季，这里相当于 autumn。

3. get a free minute：有时间。

4. best bet：最好的选择。

5. by then：到那个时候。

More Expressions（触类旁通）

1. We will attend the Frankfurt Tendence Fair next month, with booth No.123.

我们会参加下个月的法兰克福展会，我们的摊位号是 123 号。

2. Have you visited the fairs in Dubai？

请问您是否参加过迪拜的展会？

3. I'm not sure if we will visit the London Fair this year.

我不确定我们今年会不会参加伦敦展。

4. Hope to see you in the trade show.

希望在展会上可以见到您。

5. You will find our new products display then.

届时您会看到我们新产品的展示。

 Q&A（深入浅出）

Question：

如果觉得自己冒犯了客户，害怕他不再联系自己，应该怎么办？

Answer：

应该委婉地写邮件联系，简单点明自己的意思即可。对冒犯之处表示歉
意，不需要过多地说明原因。如：

"I'm afraid that I may have said something that offended you. If so, I apologize.
Please forgive my mistake！"

恐怕我说了什么冒犯您的话。如果真是这样，我向您道歉，请原谅我的
错误!

75 通知客户新网站完成 New Website Inform

　　有的时候，你刚接触一个新客户，可你的网站无法访问，或者网站正在建设中，这都会给对方带来不太好的体验。很多客户甚至会主观地认为，这个公司不可信，连一个基本的网站都没有。所以当网站正式上线，或者网站修改完成后，必须通知所有客户这一情况，让有需要的客户可以浏览访问，寻找自己需要的产品或信息。

New website

To：Nicholas Brooklyn

Cc：

Bcc：

From：Joe Lo

Subject：New website

Signature: Apple Mail!

Dear Nicholas,

On the basis of talking with your colleague Linda, I was informed that you are doing a new product line of garden tools. We are interested in expanding our current business. Could you give me some more information about this story？

In addition, I am proud to declare that the construction of our new website has been accomplished. Please surf our web at your convenience. The e-catalogue could be downloaded directly. If you have interest, I will send you the member ID & password.

Thanks and best regards,

Joe

Outline（提纲挈领）

1. on the basis of：根据，基于。

2. story：这里指"内情"，而不是"故事"。

3. be proud to declare：骄傲地宣布。

4. accomplish：完工，跟 complete 意思接近。

5. member ID：会员账号。

More Expressions（触类旁通）

1. Our website is under construction.

我们的网站还在建设中。

2. We will update our company website next week.

我们下周准备更新企业网站信息。

3. Please go and visit our new web for new products for 2020.

请访问我们的网站，了解我们为 2020 年开发的新产品。

4. You could download the price list from our official website.

您可以从我们的官网下载报价表。

5. We will upload a new company profile in PPT format.

我们将会上传一个新的公司简介的幻灯片（到我们的网站）。

Q&A（深入浅出）

Question：

是否需要在公司网站上设置电子样本或报价单的下载链接？

Answer：

可以在企业网站上提供电子样本和公共报价单。浏览者看后便可对你公司的产品一目了然，在他做好筛选后再进一步联系你，效果会很好。但要注意的是，价格是公司的机密，公司的报价单是不能够把底价透露出去的，你可以在产品图片后设置数量区间和价格区间，根据客户的要求具体报价。

如果条件允许的话，对于新产品或者有客户包装的产品，要设置保护，让拥有网站用户名和密码的人浏览。这样就可以只供老客户和熟悉的客户浏览和下载最新款的产品图片和报价，将群体限制在一个可控的范围里，不会轻易泄露公司机密。

76 公司地址变更通知 Updated Company Address Inform

一旦公司地址有变，搬到新工厂或者新办公楼，都需要通过正式的邮件通知客户，以免引起麻烦。特别是对那些正在谈判磋商、开立信用证或者寄样品的客户，一旦你方地址改了而客户不知道，会产生许多不必要的麻烦。

Company address change

To : AnilShit

Cc :

Bcc :

From : Jolin Mah

Subject : Company address change

Signature: Apple Mail!

Dear Mr. Shit,

Glad to notify you beforehand that our new office will be moved to ABC Industrial Area next month. Please refer to the attached file which mapped and addressed our undated company information.

If your time is available, please pay a visit to our company during your next buying trip in China. We have a wonderful showroom with more than 2,000 square meters. And I firmly believe you would find a majority of interesting items here.

Call me or email me directly, if you have any further questions.

Kind regards,

Jolin Mah

Outline（提纲挈领）

1. notify：通知，告知。

2. beforehand：提前，预先。

3. refer to：参考，查阅。

4. map：用地图标识，map 在这里，用作动词，而不是名词"地图"。

5. firmly believe：确信无疑，坚信不疑。

More Expressions（触类旁通）

1. The condition of our new workshop became more of orderliness than ever.

我们的新车间比以前更加井然有序。

2. Our company will be moved to DEF Building next month.

我们公司下个月就会搬到 DEF 大厦。

3. The current factory here will only do the manufacturing for basic plastic parts in the near future.

在不久的将来，这边的工厂将只会生产一些基础的塑料配件。

4. We will recruit more employees for production line and assembly line in our new factory.

我们的新工厂将会招聘更多工人，用于（产品的）生产和装配。

5. Production lines will be modified accordingly in our new workshop.

在我们的新车间，生产线将会做出相应调整。

Q&A（深入浅出）

Question :

P.S. 是否是正式的用法？能否在邮件里使用？

Answer :

这属于非正式的用法，可以在邮件里使用，但仅限于熟人之间的邮件往来。如果给不熟悉的人写邮件，或者收件人的职位比较高，就尽量多用正式用法，少用缩写。

这里，P.S. 是英文单词 postscript 的缩写，意思是"附言"。它往往在邮件结尾的时候，作为备注使用的。很多情况下，与 by the way（顺便提一下）有相近之处。如下面的例文，P.S. 就是对于正文的备注。

Dear Amanda,

Could you please give me the offer sheet today？ It is of top urgency for me to check and approve it before this weekend.

P.S.：I will be on holiday tomorrow to next Wednesday.

Best regards,
Kingsley

77 邮箱地址变更通知 Email Change Inform

一旦公司变更了现有的邮箱地址，或者因为某些特殊原因要弃用原有的邮箱，都需要在第一时间出一封正式的邮件通知客户。特别是当你离职的时候，更应该通知所有的客户和供应商关于你离职的情况和接手人的联系方式，尤其是邮箱地址。

Email address change

To：Steve Potter

Cc：

Bcc：

From：Harry Lin

Subject：Email address change

Signature: Apple Mail!

Dear Steve,

Please note that my previous e-mail address harrylin@×××.com will be invalid next Friday. And you could contact with me via sales3@×××.com.

As we are divided into 5 sales divisions for different market, and I am in charge of our business in North America.

That means, I will keep servicing you and everything will be the same as usual, just the e-mail address modification. Please help to remove the past one from your contact list, and save this one.

Thanks a lot !

Best regards,
Harry Lin

Outline（提纲挈领）

1. previous email address : 过去使用的邮箱地址。

2. be divided into ： 被分成。

3. division ：部门。

4. the same as usual ：跟过去一样。

5. remove ：移除。

More Expressions（触类旁通）

1. Please help to update my email address.
请帮忙保存一下我的新电邮地址。

2. I forgot whether I had told you my new email address.
我忘了是否告诉过您我的新电邮地址。

3. Please keep in touch !
请保持联系!

4. Please find the email address for my colleague Mr. Liu in copy line, and he will handle your orders from now on.
请看抄送栏里我同事刘先生的电邮地址，从现在开始他会接手您的订单。

5. We have to modify our email address because of the new structure.

由于组织架构的改变，我们必须更改电邮地址。

 Q&A（深入浅出）

Question：

如果去一个新公司，老板给了客户信息让业务员联系，业务员应该如何与客户打招呼？

Answer：

可以直接写一封邮件给客户，告知原因和自己接手的工作及职位，并希望对方在工作中给予你支持和配合。可以跟别的内容一起写，也可以单独写一封邮件。具体内容按照下面的格式来写。

Dear Christina,

This is Susan from ABC Trading Ltd.

I would like to inform you that I am about to take over your cases from now on. Please contact me directly for any issues for current orders or pending projects. It is my pleasure to be on service of you.

Best regards,
Susan

78 病假的自动回复 Auto-reply For Sick Leave

如果你身体不舒服请了病假，应该在邮箱里设置好自动回复，以免客户有紧急的事情却找不到人。邮件中不仅要说明情况，还需要给出别的联系方式，如暂时由某某同事跟进，服务好客户。绝对不能一走了之，不闻不问，这是很不负责任的。

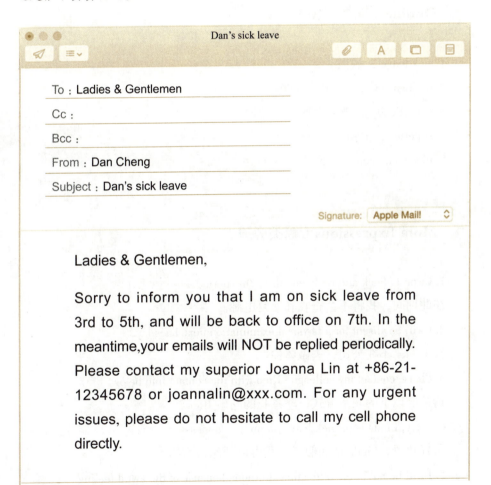

Dan's sick leave

To : Ladies & Gentlemen
Cc :
Bcc :
From : Dan Cheng
Subject : Dan's sick leave

Signature: Apple Mail!

Ladies & Gentlemen,

Sorry to inform you that I am on sick leave from 3rd to 5th, and will be back to office on 7th. In the meantime,your emails will NOT be replied periodically. Please contact my superior Joanna Lin at +86-21-12345678 or joannalin@xxx.com. For any urgent issues, please do not hesitate to call my cell phone directly.

Sorry again for the inconvenience to you !

Kind regards,
Dan Cheng

Outline（提纲挈领）

1. sick leave：病假。

2. in the meantime：在此期间。

3. periodically：规律性地，定期地。

4. superior：上司，领导。

5. inconvenience：不便。

More Expressions（触类旁通）

1. I won't check and reply emails in this period.

在此期间，我将不会查收和回复电邮。

2. I will be absent for a physical examination next Tuesday.

我下周二不在公司，去做体检。

3. Please contact my colleague Rico with the contact info below.

请按照以下的联系方式，联系我的同事 Rico。

4. Sorry, Linda is on sick leave. I can take a message for you.

不好意思，Linda 请病假了，我可以帮您留言给她。

5. I will be not in the office this afternoon because of the awful feeling.

我身体不舒服，下午将不会在办公室。

Q&A（深入浅出）

Question：

英文表达中的 hand over 和 take over 有什么区别？

Answer：

从动作上看，这两个行为是相反的。虽然都有"移交"的意思，但 hand over 侧重于"把……移交出去"；而 take over 则是"把……移交到自己手上"，有"接管、接手"的意思。你可以比较下面的例句：

My boss asked me to hand over the projects on hand.

我老板让我把手头上的项目交出来。

My boss asked me to take over the current projects from Jack.

我老板让我从 Jack 那里接手正在进行的项目。

79 宣布公司的新规定 Announcing New Office Regulations

很多时候，公司会根据业务情况的发展，修改以往的合作模式或提出新的要求等。碰到这种情况，不能简单地通知客户，还需要出具一封正式的信函。如果是重要的问题，不能放在邮件的正文里，而要使用打印签字后的扫描件，通过邮件附件形式，正式告知客户。

Anthony Wang's resignation

To : Marina Gerardo

Cc :

Bcc :

From : Ralph Lin

Subject : Anthony Wang's resignation

Signature: Apple Mail!

Hi Marina,

I formally declare that Mr. Anthony Wang has quitted since 31st Oct., 2018. We genuinely appreciate his effort and contribution to our company.

Please contact Miss Jenny Zhang from now on, for any running or pending orders which handled by Anthony formerly.

In line with my discussion with our top management, they accept to give you better payment term- O/A 45 days-with alacrity. We really hope to get more orders and cooperate closely with you.

Kind regards,

Ralph Lin

Sales Manager

Outline（提纲挈领）

1. formally declare：正式宣布。

2. genuinely：真诚地。

3. effort and contribution：努力和贡献。

4. with alacrity：十分乐意。

5. in line with：根据。

More Expressions（触类旁通）

1. I hereby announce that we will stop doing business with your company.

我在此宣布，我方将停止与贵公司的业务往来。

2. Mr. Li has left our company since 29/12/18.

李先生已在 2018 年 12 月 29 日离开了我们公司。

3. Thanks for your constant support for our business.

感谢贵公司一直以来在生意上的支持。

4. We are committed to improving our communication channel for our future orders.

我们承诺改进我方的沟通渠道，保证未来的订单顺利进行。

5. We would like to build a warehouse in Illinois for the convenient delivery in US.

我们打算在（美国）伊利诺伊州建一个仓库，以便（货物）在美国的内陆运输更加便捷。

Q&A（深入浅出）

Question：

如果不知对方是男是女，在邮件中如何称呼？

Answer：

在这种情况下，最好不要贸然猜测对方的性别，因为现在很多名字都是偏中性化的，男女都有可能使用。这个时候最好直呼其名，或者连名带姓称呼，这样不容易犯错。

另外，还要尽量去网络上搜索一下，了解名字的性别。由于很多客户并不是以英语为母语的，他们或许用丹麦语，或者挪威语，这时就很难通过名片来判断客户性别。保险起见还是通过 google 搜索，大致做个了解。

当然，也可以通过电话沟通，了解对方的性别。

80 职务调动通知 Transfer Notification

　　职场上，必然会碰到工作上的调动，可能是内部的职位调动或者升职，也可能是跳槽去别的公司，这时候就需要业务员在离开之前做好交接，明确告诉客户，你手头上的东西由谁负责跟进，后面的流程可以联系谁。业务员要为客户着想，不能留下一堆烂摊子撒手不管。

　　这是一个人的职业素养，尊重别人，也尊重自己。

Internal transfer

To : Gill Crisis

Cc :

Bcc :

From : S.M.Wei

Subject : Internal transfer

Signature: Apple Mail!

Hi Gill,

Glad to inform you that I was promoted to the team leader of our purchasing department. Ms. Fanny Tang, my assistant in the last couple of years, will hand over my work and continue doing business with you !

Thus, I really need your help to contact with her for any issues from now on. I am sure that she will pay more attention to your orders.

Thank you very much for your continued support in the past years！ I will never forget everything you have done for me！

Best wishes,
S.M. Wei

Outline（提纲挈领）

1. promote：升职，升迁。

2. team leader：团队领导者。

3. the last couple of years：过去几年。

4. thus：因此。

5. continued support：长期以来的支持。

More Expressions（触类旁通）

1. I will join in our technical department next week due to the internal transfer.
由于内部调动，从下周起我将会去我们公司的技术部门工作。

2. Mr. Zhao, my previous assistant in EU sales department, will hand over my work.
我原先的助理，欧洲业务部的赵先生，将会接手我的工作。

3. Attached please find the file for pending orders list.
附件是我们正在确认中的订单列表。

4. Here is my up-to-date contact information.

以下是我的新联系方式。

5. My email address will not be valid at the end of this month. Please contact with me via updated email address in copy line.

我旧的电邮地址在本月底就会停止使用，请通过我的新电邮地址联系我。（新电邮地址）在邮件抄送栏。

 Q&A（深入浅出）

Question：

如果你换了工作，去了一个新公司，是否方便用公司邮箱联系老客户？

Answer：

可以，但前提是，新公司有很大优势，能跟原先的老客户继续建立生意往来。如果只是投石问路，简单告诉客户，离开了老公司，去了某某公司，以打招呼为目的，或者放长线钓大鱼的，最好不要操之过急，可以先用私人邮箱联系客户，寒暄几句，告知其近况即可。

当然，邮件的正文里加上现在公司的联系方式，简单介绍几句情况，也是无可厚非的。需要注意的是，掌握好"度"，不要给客户挖墙脚的感觉，而是要让对方感觉到，你重视他，也重视他的生意，希望能给他一个更多的选择。如果有机会能够继续合作，那是你的荣幸。

81 内部工作调整通知 Internal Work Adjustment Notification

内部工作调整或者职位上的调整，在日常工作中经常会碰到。如果业务员不明确给客户相关信息，对方很容易一头雾水，给将来的工作带来不必要的麻烦。所以你在离开之前，要把事情理顺，让客户感觉不到任何的不方便，跟往常一样就可以了。

New structure of company

To : Eddie Cheung

Cc :

Bcc :

From : Kelvin Lee

Subject : New structure of company

Signature: Apple Mail!

Dear Eddie,

Sorry for the inconvenience to you. Our company spun off an EU division into a separate entity. And the initial sales department would only focus on the US orders.

It is a pity for me to begin and develop European orders from now on. And my boss Ms. Zhang will administrate the US team directly. She will contact you soon !

Thanks for your understanding.

Best regards,

Kelvin Lee

Outline（提纲挈领）

1. spin off：（从原公司或原部门中）分离，spun 是 spin 的过去式和过去分词。

2. separate entity：独立实体，这里指的是一个独立运营的部门。

3. initial：原先的，最初的。

4. focus on：专注于。

5. pity：遗憾。

More Expressions（触类旁通）

1. I will administrate our new department for R&D.

我将会（调去）管理我们新成立的市场开发部门。

2. Mr. Zhong will focus on the business for US orders independently.

钟先生将会完全独立负责我公司的美国订单。

3. Sorry to inform you that I will no longer handle your orders due to the internal transfer.

很抱歉通知您，由于内部调动，我将不再负责贵公司的订单。

4. Thanks to your constant encouragement and support.

感谢您一直以来的鼓励和支持。

5. I will never forget your relentless help.

我不会忘记您一直以来给予的帮助。

 Q&A（深入浅出）

Question：

哪些事情不适合在邮件里提及？

Answer：

日常的邮件往来，几乎涵盖了工作的方方面面，但邮件不是万能的，很多事情是不可以在邮件正文里提到的。根据笔者的工作经验，以下的内容不太适合写在邮件里。

第一，辞职后要去的新公司名或新公司联系方式。这在职场上是很忌讳的，尤其不可以还在老公司就职便告诉客户自己辞职了，以及要去的新公司名字和联系方式，这会给人非常不好的感觉。

第二，长篇大论的私人话题。公司邮箱是用来处理公务的，即使业务员跟客户私底下关系很好，可以讨论很多私人话题，但这些仅限于下班时间的交流。比如聊天工具或者私人邮箱都可以用作聊私人话题，但不可以用企业邮箱在工作时间处理私事。

第三，对同行或者竞争对手的诋毁。很多时候我们知道，同行的产品质量也许不如我们，价格也不如我们，但在商场上，这类问题可以委婉地让客户知道，不可以通过攻击别人来抬高自己，以免让人觉得无法接受。

第四，对于公司的不满或抱怨。员工在一个企业，就应当爱这份工作，所谓"做一行，爱一行"，如果做得不开心或者不满意，可以离开，但是在职的时候，对公司不满，在客户面前说公司坏话，就非常过分了。在欧美文化里，别人会认为这个人的诚信有问题。一旦诚信有了污点，对于业务员的危害是极大的。

休假通知 Annual Leave Announcement

　　休假分为两种情况，一种是个人的休假，比如年假、病假、婚假等；另一种是法定假期，或者整个公司的休假。遇到休假，要事先通知客户，并对现有的订单或跟进的项目做出交代，什么时候跟进，如何跟进，由谁负责跟进，都需要事先做好安排。

Millie's annual leave

To：Alina Stock

Cc：

Bcc：

From：Millie Yan

Subject：Millie's annual leave

Signature: Apple Mail!

Dear Alina,

I plan to start my annual leave from 25 Jul. to 4 Aug., to take my kids to enjoy our family vacation in French Polynesia. They long to see the sand beach and sea with a great view. We will transit in Tahiti airport and then to Bora Bora.

During my absence, you could reach my assistant Johnny for any issues. If anything he couldn't help you, please do not hesitate to call my mobile directly.

Thanks and best regards,
Millie

Outline（提纲挈领）

1. family vacation：家庭旅行。

2. French Polynesia：法属波利尼西亚。

3. sand beach：沙滩。

4. Tahiti：大溪地，法属波利尼西亚重要岛屿。

5. Bora Bora：波拉波拉，法属波利尼西亚重要岛屿。

More Expressions（触类旁通）

1. I am on annual leave, and will be back to office next Wednesday.

我正在休年假，下周三会回到公司。

2. Our company will be closed from Apr.3rd to 5th, because of the Tomb-sweeping Day in China.

由于清明假期，我们公司将会在 4 月 3 日到 5 日放假。

3. I am about to be on holiday from next Monday to Friday.

我下周一到周五休假。

4. Please be reminded that we will be closed for one week due to the CNY holiday.

请不要忘记我们会在中国农历新年放假一周。

5. Please note that Lily is on Sick Leave these days. You could email me directly.

请注意 Lily 最近在休病假。（有任何问题）您可以直接给我写邮件。

Q&A（深入浅出）

Question :

如何在邮件里指引对方来公司？

Answer :

除了必要的文字描述外，你还需要交代客户从哪个路口下高速，从哪里转弯，直行多少公里，在哪个红绿灯路口转弯等，还需要提供至少两位联系人的手机号码，以备不时之需，一旦客户找不到地方或者一个号码联系不上，可以得到及时的答复。

另外，附件里还需要有一张导引的草图，标注出主要的道路和公司位置，画好箭头，在文字部分配上中英文说明。因为客户需要看，驾驶员也需要看，而驾驶员有可能是中国人，所以中英文的文字对译是最理想的。

83 离职通知 Resignation Announcement

业务员因为某些原因需要离开现在的公司，走之前应该做好订单的交接，合理安排手头上的事情。另外还需要通知所有的客户、供应商，以及有业务往来的相关人员。基本的礼节是必须有的，对于帮助过你的人，不论客户、同事、朋友，还是供应商，都需要表示感谢。

Gary's resignation

To：Everybody

Cc：

Bcc：

From：Gary Liang

Subject：Gary's resignation

Signature: Apple Mail! ⬦

Dear all,

I'm sorry to inform you this is my last working day in ABC Trading. Due to some personal reasons, I will quit from tomorrow.

Thank you so much for your encouragement, help and support in the past 3 years. I cannot describe how grateful I am. Maybe someday, we could also stay together and have a drink.

I owe you the greatest debt of gratitude！ All the best！
Gary

Outline（提纲挈领）

1. all：这里指所有人。

2. last working day：最后一个工作日。

3. quit：辞职。

4. owe：欠。

5. debt of gratitude：人情债。

More Expressions（触类旁通）

1. I hope we could stay in touch！

我希望我们能保持联系！

2. I will miss you guys.

我会想你们这些家伙的。

3. I have 2 weeks off from Nov.1st to 14th.

我 11 月 1 日到 14 日会休息两周。

4. Yes, I decided to quit.

是的，我决定辞职了。

5. We are really sorry for his resignation.

我们对他的辞职表示遗憾。

Q&A（深入浅出）

Question：

如果告知客户某人离职，是否需要跟他解释原因？

Answer：

如果是因为退休而离职，需要告诉客户。如果是别的原因终止合同，或

265

者员工因为别的原因离职，是不需要告诉客户原因的，因为这属于公司内部的问题，没有必要向客户交代。只要简单告知客户，某人什么时候离职了，现在谁会接手原先的工作，联系方式是什么，就可以了。不需要画蛇添足，说一些无关痛痒的话，或者诋毁原同事，这是没有必要的。

根据欧美公司的惯例，一旦某员工离职，公司在通知客户的同时，也会对员工过去为公司做出的贡献不吝赞美，祝贺他有更好的前程。

84 退休通知 Retirement Announcement

　　某员工从公司退休，上级主管或者接手其业务的同事，应该向所有业务相关人士和内部同事做正式的邮件说明，把情况告知大家，并为将来的沟通建立通道。对于前任的贡献和表扬，也需要一并写上。

Dr. Li's retirement

To : All my colleagues & customers

Cc :

Bcc :

From : Tsui Wing On

Subject : Dr. Li's retirement

Signature: Apple Mail!

Dear all my colleagues & customers,

This is to let you know that Mr. Li Yanming, our Executive Vice President with doctorate, will leave our company as retirement soon. He will continue working until the end of August.

I assistant of Dr. Li, will take over his work from then on. We would like to thank him for the tremendous contribution & relentless support to our company in the past 15 years.

Good luck to him！

Kind regards,
Tsui Wing On
Senior Merchandise Manager

 Outline（提纲挈领）

1. retirement：退休。

2. Executive Vice President：执行副总裁。

3. doctorate：博士学位。

4. tremendous contribution：极大的贡献。

5. relentless support：一直以来的支持。

 More Expressions（触类旁通）

1. This is to let you know that Dorothy has broken the contract with our company.
在此请大家注意，Dorothy 已经跟我们公司解除了合同。

2. Mr. Wang will break the contract with us soon.
王先生很快会跟我们公司解除合同。

3. Our management vouchsafed Jack's retirement.
公司管理层批准杰克退休。

4. I expect to retire next year.
我期待明年退休。

5. I would like to express our gratitude to Dr. Zhang.
我希望在此表达我们对张博士的感激之情。

Q&A（深入浅出）

Question：

"解除合同"用英文怎么表达？

Answer：

一般有以下几种常用的表达方式：

1. break the contract

例句："He tried breaking the contract to join in our competitor's company."

译文：他千方百计想跟我们公司解除合同，跳槽去同行那边。

2. stop the contract

例句："He has stopped the contract with us."

译文：他已经跟我们中止了雇佣合同。

3. break ties with somebody

例句："We broke ties with him yesterday."

译文：我们昨天跟他解除了合同。

4. cancel the contract

例句："We have no way but to cancel the contract with you."

译文：我们没有别的办法，只有解除跟贵公司的合同。

第八天

私人往来
Personal Affairs

85 结婚通知 Marriage Announcement

结婚是人生大事，对熟悉的客户应该发邮件通知，接受他们的祝福；不熟悉的泛泛之交，也要基本通知到，让对方觉得你尊重他们。在西方文化里，这是一项基础的礼仪，不是为了让别人送礼，而是避免将来客户发现，你结婚了都没告诉他，他心里不舒服，觉得你没把他当朋友。

Marriage Announcement

To : Brad King

Cc :

Bcc :

From : Louis Cha

Subject : Marriage Announcement

Signature: Apple Mail!

Hi Brad,

I am proud to announce my marriage on 5th Jun., with my bride Miss Amy Tin. We got engaged last month when traveling in Las Vegas.

Our wedding party will be held in Hong Kong at 6 pm. We sincerely invite you to attend our ceremony.

RSVP requested！ And we could make the arrangement

in advance.

Thanks and best regards,
Louis Cha

Outline（提纲挈领）

1. proud：骄傲的，自豪的。

2. marriage：结婚，婚礼。

3. bride：新娘。

4. get engaged：订婚。

5. Las Vegas：拉斯维加斯，美国城市。

More Expressions（触类旁通）

1. We will be married next Wednesday.

我们准备在下周三结婚。

2. Please attend our engagement party next Monday.

请参加我们下周一的订婚宴。

3. Best wishes to you, the soon-to-be newlyweds.

给你们两位新人送上诚挚的祝福。

4. Glad to inform you that we are tying the knot.

很高兴通知您我们打算结婚。

5. It would be our pleasure if you could attend the wedding ceremony.

如果您能来参加我们的结婚仪式，我们将不胜荣幸。

Q&A（深入浅出）

Question：

邮件里的 RSVP 有什么含义？

Answer：

在英语中，有很多外来词和外来短语，由德语和拉丁语系衍生而来。RSVP 这个缩写本来是一个法语句子：Répondez s'il vous plaît. 翻译成汉语就是"请告诉我您是否会参加"。

在邀请函和日常商务信函里，这个短语出现的频率比较高，属于地道用法。

86 请同事们聚餐 Inviting Co-workers To Dinner Party

用一封正式的邮件对公司内部人员进行通知和邀请，会显得非常有礼貌。虽然口头的通知很必要，但邮件不可或缺，不仅可以通知时间、地点，也是对被邀请人的尊重。尤其在以英语为工作语言的公司里，由于同事之间有跨文化的代沟，这些细节一定要注意，不要给别人留下傲慢的印象。

Dinner in Shangri-La Admiralty tonight

To : All Staff

Cc :

Bcc :

From : Terry Ji

Subject : Dinner in Shangri-La Admiralty tonight

Signature: Apple Mail!

Dear All Staff,

It is my pleasure to join the team in our Hong Kong buying office. I'm sure we will make good efforts this year due to the new organizational structure with teamwork.

I faithfully invite you all for the dinner tonight in Summer Palace of Island Shangri-La Hong Kong in Pacific Place of Admiralty.

RSVP requested！

Best regards,

Terry Ji

Outline（提纲挈领）

1. it is my pleasure：这是我的荣幸。

2. new organizational structure ：新的组织架构。

3. Summer Palace：夏宫，香格里拉酒店内著名的粤餐厅。

4. Island Shangri-La Hong Kong：港岛香格里拉酒店。

5. Admiralty：金钟，香港地名。

More Expressions（触类旁通）

1. I will jump in and work with you all.

我将会参与进来跟你们一起工作。

2. I was promoted to the senior sales manager.

我被提升为高级销售经理。

3. We have a Christmas dinner every year.

我们每年都有圣诞聚餐。

4. Let us have dinner together with our new fellow.

我们跟新同事一起聚餐吧。

5. I really hope that you will have time to attend our business dinner next Friday evening.

衷心希望您有时间来参加我们下周五的商务聚餐。

Q&A（深入浅出）

Question：

如果邀请同事聚餐，邮件的抬头称谓怎么写？

Answer：

要根据实际情况分类：

第一，邀请比自己职位高的领导们一起聚餐，需要写明每个人的名字，如 Dear Mike, Jack, Nancy, Candy, and Tom ；当然也可以单独给每个领导写一封一一对应的邮件，以显尊重。

第二，邀请自己下属团队成员聚餐，可以简单写一句 Dear All Staff 或者 Dear Colleagues 即可。

第三，邀请跟自己平级的同事聚餐，比如别的部门主管，需要用适当的委婉词，如 Dear friends，显得更加亲近友好。

第四，同时邀请领导和别的同事一起聚餐，邮件就应该分开发送，领导们的邮件单独写一封，其他同事的邮件另外写一封。

此外，还要注意的是，当同时发送邮件给多人时，收件人栏的先后顺序也是要注意的。一般情况下，重要的人放在前面，按重要程度排下来，或者根据姓名英文首字母顺序排先后，以免大家产生不好的联想。

87 产子通知 Announcing The Birth Of A Child

宝宝出生后，兴奋不已的父母将这个好消息通知到同事和客户，是必要的礼貌。让别人与自己分享这份快乐，接受大家的祝福。邮件要多用 happy, excited, glad 这些表示自己兴奋的形容词，语气要委婉，不能太生硬。

Birth of my daughter

To : Everyone

Cc :

Bcc :

From : Eric Zhang

Subject : Birth of my daughter

Signature: Apple Mail!

Hello everyone,

I'm so exalted to announce the birth of my daughter Lucy on May 1st, weighted nearly 3kg. Both my wife Lily and my daughter Lucy are healthy & spry, and will be back home next week.

It is our pleasure to share this super great information to you all !

Kind regards,
Eric Zhang
On behalf of Lily

Outline（提纲挈领）

1. exalted：兴奋的，无比开心的。

2. brith：出生。

3. spry：精神不错的。

4. super great information：超级好消息。

5. on behalf of：代表。

More Expressions（触类旁通）

1. My daughter weighted nearly 2.8kg.

我女儿出生时的体重大约五斤六两。

2. It is my pleasure to announce this exciting moment.

我很高兴宣布（孩子出生）这个激动人心的时刻。

3. Both of them are doing great.

母亲和孩子都很平安。

4. The birth of our son was Nov. 22nd, 2018.

我们儿子的出生时间是 2018 年 11 月 22 日。

5. We sincerely hope you could share the fantastic message to all colleagues.

我们衷心希望您能把这个好消息告诉所有同事。

Q&A（深入浅出）

Question：

邮件的签名加上 on behalf of 是什么意思？

Answer：

在某种情况下，代替别人发的邮件，需要加以注明。如上文中，Lily 生了孩子，所以她的丈夫 Eric 代她发了邮件通知大家，这时候 Eric 只是 Lily 的代表，告知大家这个激动人心的时刻。

所以，on behalf of 可以翻译成"代表某人"，或者"以某人的名义"。

平时在工作中，如果某同事出差了，客户的邮件又很紧急，这个时候你作为同事帮忙回复，需要告知客户，因为他没有在公司，所以 email 是你代写的，而不是他本人回复的。

88 邀请客户聚餐 Inviting Customer For Lunch

如果需要给客户安排工作餐，或者特地请客户吃饭，一般需要用邮件通知并询问客户喜好。每个人的口味不同，民族和宗教文化也有差异，有人爱吃西餐，有人想吃中餐，有人喜欢日韩料理，有人不吃生冷食物。因此，需要事先跟客户打好招呼，得到确认才能安排或订位。贸然自作主张，会引起对方不快。

Buying trip with lunch

To : Mario Brown

Cc :

Bcc :

From : Lina Chu

Subject : Buying trip with lunch

Signature: Apple Mail!

Dear Mario,

Thank you for your buying trip schedule in detail. We will arrange the pickup in the lobby at 9 am tomorrow morning. Is it viable for one 7-passenger minivan？Do you have many trolley cases of luggage？

By the way, it takes roughly 2 hours to drive from the hotel to our factory. And we invite you to have lunch in advance, and then visit our showroom & workshop.

Do you prefer Chinese, Japanese or Western style？

We recommend a nice restaurant for French Teppanyaki to you. And another Japanese restaurant for Kaiseki Ryori is also very good.

Please advise us of your option, and we could arrange it accordingly.

Thanks and best regards,
Lina Chu

Outline（提纲挈领）

1. lobby：酒店大堂。

2. 7-passenger minivan：七座商务车。

3. trolley case：拉杆箱。

4. French Teppanyaki：法式铁板烧。

5. Kaiseki Ryori：怀石料理，属于日餐中顶级的料理。

More Expressions（触类旁通）

1. We will arrange a quick working lunch tomorrow.

我们明天会安排好快捷的工作餐。

2. Would you like to have some aperitif？

你想来点开胃酒吗？

3. We arranged some French minced garlic bread as afternoon tea.

我们准备了一些法式蒜蓉面包做下午茶。

4. A cup of espresso？

要来杯意式浓缩咖啡吗？

5. We booked a dish of salmon sashimi for you.

我们给您叫了一份三文鱼刺身。

Q&A（深入浅出）

Search

Question：

法餐和日料中的 Teppanyaki 是什么意思？

Answer：

Teppanyaki 可以翻译为铁板烧，是近些年非常流行的一种即食料理，在日本非常出名，食材和价格比传统的日本料理要高出一个档次，做铁板烧的餐厅以高档餐厅居多。主要采用高品质的海鲜、肉类、蔬菜等，由专业的料理师在铁板上现煎，同时只添加少许的盐、胡椒和酱汁，保持食物的原汁原味。

高档的 Teppanyaki 一般都价格不菲，往往用来宴请重要客户，有别于相对快餐式的 Okonomiyaki（大阪烧）。地道的日式铁板烧餐厅，一块日本和牛的价格甚至可能高达千元人民币。

Teppanyaki 的历史可以追溯到 15 世纪的西班牙，但真正在世界餐饮行业发扬光大的，则只有 Japanese Teppanyaki（日式铁板烧）和 French Teppanyaki（法式铁板烧）这两种。

89 跟客户讨论私人问题 Private Conversation With Customer

很多客户不喜欢在工作的邮件里讨论私人问题，但也有少部分客户跟供应商熟悉以后，也能像朋友一样交流，工作之余聊些私人话题，增进彼此间的感情。

笔者的个人意见是，不主动讨论跟工作无关的事，以免让对方觉得自己不专业。当然，偶尔的一句问候或几句寒暄，就另当别论了。如果是客户提出一些私人问题，方便的情况下就需要认真回答，因为这是跟客户拉近距离的好机会，不容错过。

Traveling plan to Europe

To : Lucia Garibaldi

Cc :

Bcc :

From : Nancy Zhu

Subject : Traveling plan to Europe

Signature: Apple Mail!

Dear Lucia,

Thanks for your invitation to Italy ! I plan to attend the trade show in Paris first, and then fly to Milan directly, with my husband and daughter. We will pick a car from Hertz, and then travel to Florence and Venice by self-driving for one week.

Ah, could you please help me to check the shopping outlets near Florence or Venice？ We wanna buy some Prada and Gucci here.

We will fly to Rome on 25th Feb. I really want to see you then！ Give you a hug！

Best regards,
Nancy

Outline（提纲挈领）

1. Hertz：赫兹，国际著名租车公司。
2. Florence：佛罗伦萨，意大利著名城市，文艺复兴起源地。
3. Venice：威尼斯，意大利旅游城市。
4. self-driving：自驾。
5. hug：拥抱。

More Expressions（触类旁通）

1. Please book Residenza Paolo VI Hotel for us in Roma.
请帮忙给我们预定罗马的保罗六世公寓酒店。
2. Shall we pay a visit to your stores then？
我们那时候能否来拜访一下你们的店铺？
3. Could you help us to get 2 train tickets？
能帮我们买两张火车票吗？

4. What is the most convenient routine from Barcelona to Prague ?

从（西班牙）巴塞罗那到（捷克）布拉格，怎么走最方便？

5. I applied for the Schengen Visa to roam in a lot of European countries.

我申请了去欧洲多国旅行的申根签证。

Q&A（深入浅出）

Question：

什么是 Schengen Visa（申根签证）？

Answer：

做外贸的朋友们经常会去欧洲参展或者拜访客户，申根签证是必须准备的。如果单纯去一个国家，如德国或者法国，那可以去德国或法国驻华领事馆，办理只去该国的"国别签证"。但若临时改变行程，或者顺道拜访其他国家的客户，就不那么方便了。

根据 1985 年在卢森堡小镇申根（Schengen）签订的协议，德国、法国、比利时、荷兰、卢森堡五国互相规定，对短期逗留者颁发一种可以随时进入这五个国家的签证，这就是申根签证的雏形。

到今天，已经有 26 个成员承认和签发申根签证。只要在签证有效期内，就可以随时进入和离开这些国家，这对前往欧洲的商务人士是一种极大的便利。

关于 Schengen Visa 的详情，请参阅网址：http：//www.schengenvisa.cc/.

90 请客户帮忙 Seeking For Helping Hand

　　业务员工作中常常会碰到各种麻烦，如果正巧客户举手之劳便能解决，还是需要委婉地请求他帮助。当然，如果事情很棘手，业务员跟客户的关系还没有到那一步，就要尽量独立处理，避免去麻烦别人。

Seeking for helping hand

To : Sophie Carpenter

Cc :

Bcc :

From : Jessica Wang

Subject : Seeking for helping hand

Signature: Apple Mail! ↕

Sophie,

I'm sorry to bother you.

I got acquainted with a new customer in Las Vegas fair, for gardening tools. She would like to get some more info about our company, our running projects and our current US customers.

Shall I transfer your email address and phone number to her？ Maybe she will dial you directly to know the ropes from your side. Could you put in a good words for me？

Thanks and best regards,
Jessica

 Outline（提纲挈领）

1. bother：打扰，麻烦。

2. get acquainted with somebody：结识某人。

3. running projects：进行中的项目。

4. know the ropes：了解内情。

5. put in a good words：说好话。

 More Expressions（触类旁通）

1. Shall we put your company name on our profile PPT？
能把贵公司的名字放入我们企业简介的幻灯片上吗？

2. Please advise the suggested retail price.
请告知一下"建议零售价"。

3. In other words, your helping hand could help us to expand the Benelux market.
换言之，您的帮助能让我们迅速扩大（我们的产品）在比利时、荷兰和卢森堡的市场。

4. We could offer a helping hand if you face the payment problems.
如果贵公司在支付方面碰到麻烦，我们愿意提供帮助。

5. Could you book the round trip air ticket and hotel for me in the period of Hong Kong fair？

能否帮我订一下香港展会期间的往返机票和酒店？

 Q&A（深入浅出）

Question：

如何理解 Northern Europe market 和 Scandinavian market 的差异？

Answer：

其实，真正意义上的北欧国家有五个，分别是 Denmark（丹麦），Norway（挪威），Finland（芬兰），Sweden（瑞典）和 Iceland（冰岛）。严格意义上的 Northern Europe market，就是指这五个国家。

但是这里面，除了冰岛孤悬海外，其他四个国家，都在斯堪的纳维亚半岛上，文化、地域和经济水平都十分接近，所以 Scandinavian market，往往就是我们所谓的狭义的"北欧市场"，就是北欧四国，不包含冰岛在内。

如果单独提 Northern Europe market，就是包含冰岛在内的北欧五国市场。

第九天

特别问候
Special Greetings

91 圣诞问候 X'mas Greetings

对于许多西方国家而言，圣诞节是一年中的头等节日，相当于中国的农历新年。一般圣诞节前，很多客户都会开始安排放假，有些客户甚至会放长假到元旦以后的许多天。为了避免耽搁工作，紧急的问题需要提早在圣诞节前跟客户确认好，同时询问一下对方放假的时间，并给予节日祝福。

X'mas greetings

To：Camy Linter

Cc：

Bcc：

From：Teddy Huang

Subject：X'mas greetings

Signature: Apple Mail!

Dear Camy,

Glad to hear that your company will be closed from 22nd Dec. to 28th Dec. for X'mas holiday.

Thank you so much for your directions and support as always. Please enjoy the family time during this optimal holiday, together with the boxing day.

Best regards,
Teddy

Outline（提纲挈领）

1. X'mas：圣诞，是 Christmas 的缩写。

2. directions：指点。

3. as always：一如既往。

4. optimal：最佳的，最理想的。

5. boxing day：节礼日。

More Expressions（触类旁通）

1. Please enjoy your holiday and celebrate the Christmas.

请好好享受您的假期，并庆祝圣诞。

2. I wish you all the best.

祝您一切顺心。

3. Please accept our wholehearted X'mas greetings.

请接受我们由衷的圣诞祝福。

4. Season's greetings！

圣诞快乐!

5. We hope you will get everything your heart desires.

祝您心想事成。

Q&A（深入浅出）

Question：

wholehearted 这个词应如何理解?

Answer：

在英文的祝福语中，这个单词出现频率很高，可以翻译为"全心全意的""由衷的""真心的"等，用来强调后面的 congratulations（祝贺）或 greetings（祝福）。如：

1. "Please take my wholehearted congratulations to Jimmy, on his promotion."
请给吉米带去我由衷的祝贺，祝贺他升职。

2. "Despite our hard work and wholehearted enthusiasm, we finally lost the order from Disney."
尽管我们努力工作、满腔热情，但最终还是没有拿下迪士尼的订单。

92 新年问候 New Year Greetings

　　新年问候通常会跟圣诞问候放在一起，但是也有很多客户不过圣诞节，比如中东地区的、欧美地区的犹太人等，对于这类客户，只要简单地道以新年祝福就可以了。所以发送圣诞祝福或者圣诞贺卡之前一定要弄清楚，客户是否会过圣诞节，画蛇添足就不好了。

New Year greetings

To : Christina Reno

Cc :

Bcc :

From : Edison C.

Subject : New Year greetings

Signature: Apple Mail!

Dear Christina,

Kindly note I will be absent from 1st to 3rd Jan., on account of the New Year's holiday.

For any emergencies, please call my mobile phone or send me short message.

Happy New Year ! Hope it brings you more success and happiness !

Kind regards,
Edison C.

Outline（提纲挈领）

1. on account of：由于，因为。

2. New Year's holiday：元旦假期。

3. emergencies：紧急事件。

4. short message：短信。

5. success and happiness：成功与幸福，英文中，这两个词常放在一起用。

More Expressions（触类旁通）

1. Please enjoy your holiday and celebrate Christmas.

请好好享受您的假期，并庆祝圣诞。

2. May success and happiness in the coming New Year！

祝您在新的一年里有更多的成功与欢乐！

3. Happy New Year！ My dear friend！

我亲爱的朋友，祝你新年快乐！

4. Greetings on your CNY holiday！

祝您农历新年假期快乐！

5. On behalf of our sales department, I wish you all a happy new year.

我代表我们公司业务部全体同事，祝你们新年快乐！

Q&A（深入浅出）

Question：

看似接近的两个表达，"I wish you a happy new year" 和 "I wish you Happy New Year" 意思是否相同？

Answer：

这两句话的意思完全不同，不能乱用，一定要小心。

"I wish you a happy new year." 这句话的意思是祝您新的一年快乐，侧重点是整个的一年，而不是新年的一天或者几天的假期。

"I wish you Happy New Year." 这句话的意思是祝您新年快乐，没有侧重一整年，而是指新年这个假期。在地道的英文表达里，这个用法非常罕见，似乎在语感上缺少了一点说不清、道不明的东西，还不如简单的一句 Happy New Year 来得直接。

93 春节问候 Chinese New Year Greetings

　　对我们中国人而言，春节往往是一年中最重要的假期，需要跟家人团聚，来享受一年中最悠闲的时光。可休息归休息，工作的事情还是需要交代好。对于供应商、客户，以及生意上往来的各类朋友，都需要告知他们你春节的放假情况，并对他们表示祝福。

Chinese New Year greetings

To : All

Cc :

Bcc :

From : Spencer Feng

Subject : Chinese New Year greetings

Signature: Apple Mail!

Ladies & Gentlemen,

Our office will be closed down during the Chinese New Year period from 2nd Feb. to 9th Feb. And we will get back into harness on 10th.

Any pending cases will be disposed thereafter. I'm sorry we cannot figure out everything before the holiday.

Wishing you all a Happy New Year !

Best regards,
Spencer Feng

Outline（提纲挈领）

1. close down：停工。

2. get back into harness：重回工作岗位。

3. dispose：处理。

4. thereafter：从那以后。

5. figure out：解决。

More Expressions（触类旁通）

1. All the goods will be shipped before the CNY holiday.

所有的货都会在春节前出运。

2. I'm afraid that the last order will be delivered after the CNY holiday.

恐怕最后一个订单要在春节后出货了。

3. Sorry to inform you the goods have to be postponed 3 shipments, because of the labor shortage in the period of CNY holiday.

由于春节期间劳动力缺乏，很抱歉通知您，货需要延期三个航次。

4. It is our peak season before the CNY holiday.

春节前是我们最忙的时候。

5. Please settle the payment before our CNY holiday. Thank you！

请在我们春节放假前付款，谢谢！

Q&A（深入浅出）

Question：

Spring Festival 和 Chinese New Year 是否同义？

Answer：

可以理解为近义。两者都表示中国的农历新年，也就是春节。但有的时候，Spring Festival 还可以单独表示农历的"正月初一"。

如果是春节假期，Spring Festival 可以单独表达，而 Chinese New Year 后面就需要加上 holiday 这个单词。

94 感恩节问候 Thanksgiving Day Greetings

　　感恩节是美国的全国性节日，盛行于美国和加拿大。感恩节到圣诞节的这一个多月，美国零售业的销售额能占据全年销售额的三分之一，是商家打折促销的旺季。所以感恩节前夕，可以给美国零售商一个问候，预祝他生意兴隆。但必须注意，感恩节不是欧美共有，欧洲没有感恩节，千万不能向欧洲人祝贺，那是非常不礼貌的！

Thanksgiving Day greetings

To : Craig James

Cc :

Bcc :

From : Steve Jin

Subject : Thanksgiving Day greetings

Signature: Apple Mail!

Hi Craig,

Thanksgiving Day is coming. On behalf of all staff in our company, I wish you a huge retail in the holiday season of Thanksgiving Day and Christmas.

If anything we can give assistance, you may just speak to me.

Good luck！ May you be happy and prosperous！

Kind regards,
Steve Jin

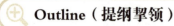 **Outline（提纲挈领）**

1. Thanksgiving Day：感恩节，美国节日，欧洲没有。

2. all staff：所有员工。

3. a huge retail：零售暴涨。

4. give assistance：从旁协助。

5. prosperous：繁荣的，兴旺的。

More Expressions（触类旁通）

1. Thanksgiving Day is coming.

感恩节快要到了。

2. Obviously, the sales forecast for Thanksgiving Day holiday will be awesome.

很明显今年感恩节假期的销售情况会非常棒。

3. Shall we have Thanksgiving dinner together？

我们能一起用感恩节晚餐吗？

4. I plan to go around in Macy's, to find some interesting items.

我计划去梅西百货逛逛，找一些有意思的东西。

5. Do you have promotion plan before Thanksgiving Day？

你们在感恩节前夕有促销计划吗？

Q&A（深入浅出）

Question：

Thanksgiving Day（感恩节）的由来是什么？

Answer：

感恩节的历史可以追溯到 17 世纪，当时在英国受到迫害的清教徒们，逃离英国本土，漂洋过海来到美洲大陆，许多人都死在途中及美洲大陆。这个时候，美洲土著印第安人给了这些活下来的移民帮助，提供了生活必需品并教他们生存方式。所以感恩节的由来，一大部分是为了感谢印第安人的慷慨赠予和帮助。

从 19 世纪开始，感恩节就确定为每年 11 月第四个礼拜的周四，这一天是美国人家人团聚和举国欢庆的日子，有点类似于中国人的中秋节，在美国是一个相当传统且有着悠久历史的节日。

然而感恩节仅适用于美国和加拿大，跟欧洲人是没有关系的，他们不会去感谢远在大西洋彼岸的印第安人，所以欧洲没有感恩节，也不会有感恩节假期。对欧洲客户致以感恩节的问候，是非常不礼貌甚至会适得其反的！

在美国，感恩节和圣诞节这两个假期挨得很近，也是美国人一年中的购物旺季，很多商场和百货公司都会选择在这个时候打折和促销，来吸引消费者。不论是节日准备也好，亲朋好友之间赠礼也罢，对商家而言，都是一个很好的销售季节。

关于感恩节的具体由来，请参阅以下网页：

"http：//en.wikipedia.org/wiki/Thanksgiving."

95 万圣节问候 Halloween Greetings

每年的 10 月 31 日，是西方世界的主要节日之一，万圣节（Halloween）。万圣节起源于欧洲传统的鬼节，几个世纪以来，逐渐转化为今天孩子们的节日。

每到这一天，孩子们就会穿着奇装异服，装扮成各种恐怖的形象，挨家挨户敲门要糖。这一天是孩子们一年中尽情欢乐的日子。万圣节前夕，给客户道一声祝福，或者送给他的孩子一些小礼物，效果都是非常好的。

Halloween greetings

To : Andy Johnson

Cc :

Bcc :

From : Daniel Xu

Subject : Halloween greetings

Signature: Apple Mail!

Dear Andy,

Have you prepared the sales planning for Halloween pumpkin, together with other party items in the same category？ Hope all the items have already been hit the shelves in the stores.

An updated sample has been sent out to you by FedEx. Maybe you could try to place orders next year. I also bought some interesting Halloween gifts and

---

put them into the same parcel. Please help to transfer them to your kids.

All the best !
Daniel Xu

Outline（提纲挈领）

1. sales planning：销售计划。
2. pumpkin：南瓜。
3. party items：节日礼品。
4. hit the shelves：（产品）上架。
5. transfer：这里指"转交"。

More Expressions（触类旁通）

1. Do you have interest in purchasing some Halloween costume ?
请问您有没有兴趣采购一些万圣节装束？

2. Please attend our Halloween party next Monday in Lan Kwai Fong.
请参加我们下周一在香港兰桂坊的万圣节酒会。

3. We will hold a Halloween banquet in Peninsula Hong Kong.
我们会在香港半岛酒店举行万圣节晚宴。

4. Halloween is the holiday for your kids.
万圣节是你的孩子们的节日。

5. What is your aim in the sales season of Halloween ?
万圣节期间你打算如何销售？

Q&A（深入浅出）

Question：

万圣节（Halloween）是怎么来的？

Answer：

万圣节跟感恩节不同，不仅是美洲大陆的节日，也是欧洲地区、澳大利亚和新西兰等国的重要节日。在西方，11 月 1 日是传统意义上的 "All Hollow's Day"（天下圣徒之日），而其前夜就是 Halloween，跟圣诞节前夜的 Christmas Eve 是同样的道理。

万圣节起源于古英伦三岛的凯尔特人（Celtics），在他们的信仰里，新的一年从每年的 11 月 1 日开始，而死亡之神会带领鬼魂们，在 10 月 31 日晚上重返人间，寻找替身。所以他们点燃火炬，用奇装异服装扮自己，让鬼魂们认不出自己，逃过灾难。后来，万圣节就慢慢从不列颠和欧洲诸国，传到美洲大陆和大洋洲等地。

如今，万圣节逐渐褪去宗教色彩，转变为一个让孩子们欢乐的节日。他们可以穿各种衣服，打扮成任何想要装扮的样子，如僵尸、吸血鬼、恶魔等，挨家挨户敲门要糖，尽情欢乐。

关于 Halloween（万圣节）的更多信息，请参阅以下网页：

"http：//en.wikipedia.org/wiki/Halloween."

96 长假问候 Holiday Greetings

海外客户每年除了公共假期外，还会留出一定的时间休年假，跟家人一起旅行或者好好休息一阵子。欧美客户一般会选择七八月份最热的时候，去中东、马尔代夫、摩纳哥等地度假旅行。短的可能一周，长的甚至会两个月。

最好不要在假期的时候打扰客户，谈工作上的事情。假期结束后，联系工作的同时，也要适当问候一下他假期的情况。

Holiday greetings

To : Mathias Ferguson

Cc :

Bcc :

From : Emily Chen

Subject : Holiday greetings

Signature: Apple Mail!

Dear Mathias,

I'm so chuffed to hear that you will take a holiday to Maldives next week. I enjoyed a couple of weeks there in St.Regis and Conrad. That was extraordinarily amazing ! I'm sure you will love the water bungalow there.

Back to the business, when will you come back to office？ I want to talk to you for the pending order for

Disney.

Have a nice trip and enjoy your holiday！

Best regards,
Emily Chen

Outline（提纲挈领）

1. chuffed ：高兴的。

2. Maldives ：马尔代夫，著名旅行圣地。

3. extraordinarily ：非凡地，出众地。

4. water bungalow ：水上屋。

5. back to the business ：言归正传。

More Expressions（触类旁通）

1. I'm on Annual Leave in Bali, and will resume work next Tuesday.

我正在巴厘岛休年假，下周二会回去工作。

2. I remember the first time I told you I was going on vacation.

我记得我第一时间就告诉过你我要去休假了。

3. Holidaymakers like go traveling to Dubai in July.

度假的人们喜欢 7 月去迪拜。

4. It is the Bank Holiday today in the UK.

今天是英国的公众假期。

5. He was on holiday and we hadn't got any approval for the delivery time.

他那时候在度假，我们在这之前没有收到过任何船期方面的确认。

Q&A（深入浅出）

Question：

如何用英语形容一个不休假的工作狂?

Answer：

工作狂在欧美是一个中性词，一方面赞扬这个人工作上的努力，另一方面也觉得这人相对古板且不懂得休闲。英语中有两个近义词，一个是 workaholic，另一个是 ergasiomania。相对来说，前者更有赞扬的意思，后者的狂热程度更深，给人的印象不是太好。因为 aholic 理解为"沉迷于……的人"，而 mania 这个单词的意思则偏向于"狂热、狂躁"。试看以下例句：

1. "The guy is a workaholic. He works all year around without a holiday."

这个家伙是个工作狂，他一年到头工作都不用休假。

2. "My boss is an crazy ergasiomania, who works from dawn till midnight and never gives himself a weekend."

我老板是个地地道道的工作狂，每天一早工作到半夜，连周末都从来不休息。

97 祝贺新婚 Marriage Celebrating

特别熟悉或者私交甚好的客户，有时会跟供应商谈一些私人话题，比如结婚之类的。你一定要在得到信息的第一时间，写邮件或打电话表示祝贺。如果时间及其他方面允许，还应该尽量参加婚礼或准备一份小礼物。

Marriage Celebrating

To : Mandy Hilton

Cc :

Bcc :

From : Jacqueline Cha

Subject : Marriage Celebrating

Signature: Apple Mail!

Dear Mandy,

We are thrilled and delighted to know about your marriage with Jack in Seattle next Saturday.

All our team members of No.2 Sales Division intend to send you a tiny gift with congratulations. Please also extend our regards to your husband.

Our sales rep Lynn is going to attend your wedding party then. She will stay at Fairmont Olympic Hotel in Seattle.

Kind regards,
Jacqueline Cha

Outline（提纲挈领）

1. thrilled：极为激动的。

2. Seattle：西雅图。

3. intend：打算，计划。

4. sales rep：销售代表。

5. Fairmont：费尔蒙酒店，国际著名酒店集团，是法国雅高国际酒店集团旗下品牌。

More Expressions（触类旁通）

1. I'm so pleased to receive your wedding invitation.

我非常高兴收到您的结婚请帖。

2. Tom and Betty begin their married life.

汤姆和贝蒂开始了他们的婚姻生活。

3. Congratulations on your engagement！

祝贺你们订婚!

4. Glad to hear that you got engaged.

很高兴获悉你们已经订婚了。

5. How joyful to hear that you plan to marry up！

听说你们准备结婚，这太让人高兴了!

Q&A（深入浅出）

Question：

"to get married"和"get married to"是否是一个意思？

Answer：

不太一样，前者代表"结婚"，强调状态，后者表示"与某人结婚"，强调动作。试看以下例句：

1. "Mary wants to get married to live in US."

玛丽想要通过结婚，达到定居美国的目的。

2. "She got married to an American guy."

她跟一个美国人结婚了。

另外，表示结婚的状态也可以用 marry up；表示与某人结婚可以直接用 marry somebody。英文中还有一个短语 marry into money，可以形象地翻译成"傍大款"。

98 祝贺升职 Promotion Celebrating

升职、加薪，往往是职场中最值得高兴的事。一旦得知客户在公司的职位有升迁，应第一时间表示祝贺，感谢其在过去工作中的帮助和支持，也对未来的合作表示进一步的信心。很多跨国公司的管理非常严谨，一旦某某人升职，都会由直属上司或人力资源部门撰写相关通知邮件，抄送全球所有供应商及合作伙伴。

Congratulations

To : Edmund Messi

Cc :

Bcc :

From : May Li

Subject : Congratulations

Signature: Apple Mail!

Dear Edmund,

Congratulations on your promotion to Senior Category Manager of Asia Pacific Hub.

I know beyond a doubt that you deserve this honor due to your full experience in procurement and administration.We really appreciate your help and trust in the past years. We will always remember your kindliness.

> Back to the business, could you please advise which guy will hand over your work as buying head？Abraham or Mason？
>
> Best regards,
>
> May Li

Outline（提纲挈领）

1. Senior Category Manager：高级品类经理。

2. Asia Pacific Hub：亚太区总部。

3. know beyond a doubt：确信无疑。

4. deserve this honor：受之无愧，当之无愧。

5. kindliness：亲切，友好。

More Expressions（触类旁通）

1. Congratulations on your promotion！

恭喜你升职!

2. Will you be promoted to QC manager？

你将被提升为验货主管吗?

3. We're pleased to hear that you were named managing director in Asia Pacific region.

我们很高兴获悉你被提升为亚太区总裁。

4. My assistant Linda will hand over my current business with you after my promotion.

我升职以后，我助理琳达会接手我手上跟贵公司合作的生意。

5. You deserve it！

你当之无愧!

 Q&A（深入浅出）

Question：

"You deserve it！"能否用来夸奖别人升职?

Answer：

这是可以的。英文中，deserve 这个单词有"值得、应得"的意思。别人获得升迁，恭喜的时候，愉快而坚定地说一句"You deserve it！"，就是给对方最大的夸奖，"这是你应得的！""你当之无愧！"之类的话能让对方很开心。这句话可以用于口语，也可以用于如今日趋口语化的英文书信。

但世事无绝对，一句话的准确表达同样要依赖不同的语境。如果一个同事正巧做错了事，挨了老板的骂，还被扣了奖金，而另一个同事在旁边阴阳怪气地说了句"You deserve it！"，那意思就完全变味了，就变成充满讽刺的"活该！"或"自找的!"

99 敬祝早日康复 Get-well Messages

得知客户生病，礼节上应该写封私人邮件慰问一下，不论他是否已经康复。不需要太长，简单几句话点明主旨就可以。这封邮件是以鼓励和关怀为目的，不是万不得已的情况下，不应该出现跟工作有关的事宜。

Get-well message

To：Howard Bryant

Cc：

Bcc：

From：Liam Liu

Subject：Get-well message

Signature: Apple Mail!

Dear Howard,

We learned from your assistant that you had been hospitalized. All of us here are hoping your recovery asap.

Don't worry about any pending cases. We will control everything well and keep in touch with your colleagues. You have my word. We can fix all the problems.

Get well soon. God bless you！

Best regards,
Liam Liu

Outline（提纲挈领）

1. learn from：从某处获悉。

2. hospitalize：住院。

3. recovery：康复，痊愈。

4. You have my word：我保证。

5. get well soon：尽快好起来。

More Expressions（触类旁通）

1. Sorry to hear about your illness.

很遗憾得知您生病了。

2. We felt so bad to learn that you had been hospitalized.

得知您生病住院，我们非常担心。

3. We're praying your quick recovery.

我们会祈祷您尽快康复。

4. What a shock it was to hear about your father's serious illness！

得知令尊病重，不胜震惊！

5. God bless you！

愿上帝保佑您!

Q&A（深入浅出）

Question：

怎么跟客户说"早日康复"？

Answer：

在英文中，如果需要直译，可以说一句"Get well soon!"，就是祝对方尽早康复的意思。同时也可以用一些委婉的表达，比如"May God bless you!"（愿上帝保佑你！）或者"Hope to see you up and around asap."（希望很快就见你活蹦乱跳），也可以简单说句"Take Care"（注意身体）！

100 寄送小礼物 Sending Out A Tiny Gift

在欧美人的观念里，一份小礼物往往代表客户或朋友的一份心意，礼物不在于贵重，可以是一枝玫瑰、一小盒巧克力、一碟自制的小饼干、一双棉手套等。如果价值过高，反而会让对方有压力，觉得欠了人情，或者没有办法接受。所以我们给欧美客户送礼，也要从文化的角度尽量为对方考虑。

A tiny gift

To : Jeremy Colin

Cc :

Bcc :

From : Michelle Zhao

Subject : A tiny gift

Signature: Apple Mail!

Dear Jeremy,

I am so gratified to hear that you are going to Hong Kong Disney with your daughter for her birthday next week. I just prepared a tiny gift for her, a tin of cartoon handmade biscuits.

Shall we have a dinner together if you have time then？ What about the Thai food restaurant near the Victoria Peak？

319

I look forward to hearing from you soon.

Best regards,
Michelle Zhao

 Outline（提纲挈领）

1. gratified：高兴的，满意的。

2. a tiny gift：一件小礼物。

3. cartoon handmade biscuits：卡通手工饼干。

4. Thai food：泰国菜。

5. Victoria Peak：香港太平山顶。

 More Expressions（触类旁通）

1. We could arrive at the restaurant by Peak Tram.
我们可以坐缆车到达太平山顶的餐厅。

2. I plan to go around in Taipei 101 and bring a tiny gift for my girlfriend.
我打算去台北 101 逛逛，给我女朋友带个小礼物。

3. I redeemed my promise to visit you in Argentina and bring a tiny gift.
我履行了我的承诺，来阿根廷看你，并带了一个小礼物。

4. A tiny gift has been sent to you by UPS.
（我）已经通过联合包裹寄给你了一个小礼物。

5. Please transfer the gifts and extend my regards to your kids.
请帮忙把礼物转交给您的孩子们，并送去我的祝福。

Q&A（深入浅出）

Question：

如果给客户快递一份小礼物，是否可以让对方到付运费？

Answer：

不可以！因为礼物是表示一份心意，如果让对方承担运费，就失去了送礼的本意。给客户或者其家人孩子送一个小礼物，本身是拉近彼此的距离，礼物不需要多贵，可以是一个小毛绒玩具，或者一套小文具，送给他的孩子，都是非常好的。如果让对方承担运费，反而会适得其反，让对方不快，甚至反感。

也有朋友问，如果本来就要给客户寄样品，是不是可以把小礼物跟样品一起快递过去？我的回答依然是否定的。在欧美人观念里，公是公，私是私。给他寄样品，不论是预付还是到付，都是工作上的事情。而给他孩子寄个小礼物，那属于私事，要另当别论。甚至有些客户很讨厌在工作中处理私事，如果要快递礼物，最好直接快递到家。

第十天

细节问题
Issues In Detail

101 附件的问题 Attachment Issue

英文电邮，经常会用到附件。邮件里没法简单说明的需要用附件，图片文件需要用附件，报价单需要用附件，测试报告需要用附件，相关图稿需要用附件，产品的技术参数需要用附件，多品类比对需要用附件。

既然附件有如此多的用处，那如何把附件用好、用巧、用妙，锦上添花，而不画蛇添足，能发挥长处，而不是自爆短板，就相当重要了。

不要忘记插入附件

这是个老生常谈的问题，大家都可能会忘记插入附件，我也会忘。明明邮件里写了，"Please find the price list in attachment." 结果发送的时候还是忘记把附件插入。运气好的，也许发送以后很快就发现，再跟进一封邮件加上附件，虽然不是太好但也无伤大雅。不太仔细的，就是发了以后自己也不知道，等客户回复："附件呢？"才猛然想起，自己忘记插入了，这是非常尴尬的，会让对方觉得你不专业。

所以在每封邮件发送之前，自己一定要通读一下，看看是否通顺简洁、没有歧义，是否忘记加入附件。

附件不能过大

附件的大小是需要严格控制的，简单来说，如果不是用来做设计稿或者印刷稿确认，是不需要使用太大的附件的。很多业务员给客户做报价单，总是顺手把刚拍好的照片插入 excel，结果造成文件过大，好几兆甚至几十兆，发送的人吃力，客户收取也麻烦，浪费彼此时间，还要挑战客户耐心，何苦呢！

所以在制作报价单的时候，插入图片之前可以先用 photoshop 做好处理，修边、设置图片大小、修改像素、图片压缩，让每张照片都显示成同样大小和同样尺寸，再放进报价单里，一眼看上去非常整洁美观，体现出自己的专业和在细节上的把控。

附件里多张同类图片尽量合并

有的时候，客户可能需要业务员发送一些产品图片，在客户没有指向性的情况下，可能要发很多张图片。如果一股脑儿插入几十张 jpg 文件，即便都经过压缩处理，还是会让附件看起来很杂乱。也有业务员习惯把这些文件打成压缩包，然后作为附件发送。但是很不幸，根据笔者多年从业经验，大部分客户是打不开也不会使用压缩包文件的，不会解压缩。所以尽量少用压缩文件作为附件发送。老客户还好，一般会说一声，附件打不开，让你重新发一遍。如果是新客户，也许打不开，就直接删了。

这种情况下，笔者个人的意见是，把多张图片合成一份 PDF 文件，控制一下尺寸，这样客户就可以像翻书一样，一页一页浏览过去，比一张一张点开、关闭，要方便许多。

还有更多关于图片方面的问题，请看下节的详细表述。

附件过多可以分开发送

一旦有很多附件要同时发送，比如报价单、测试报告、验厂报告、产品说明书、产品详细图片、包装图片、标贴图片、外箱唛头图片等，可以归类以后，分几封邮件发送。假设产品是一款太阳能灯，就可以分成以下几封邮件，设置不同主题。

第一封邮件，只发报价单和产品图片、包装图片，侧重点是产品。邮件主题可以设置为：Offer sheet & photos for solar light。

第二封邮件，突出的是自身的产品特点，那说明书、产品测试报告，就可以放在这封邮件里，把主题设置成 Instruction manual & testing report for solar light。

第三封邮件，突出自身的工厂条件，发一些工厂图片、样品间图片、验厂报告，给客户一个整体的印象，主题设置成 Factory audit report and showroom photos。

第四封邮件，提供一些细节的东西，比如不干胶标贴、吊卡、彩盒设计稿、外箱唛头等，作为补充，主题设置成 Artwork draft for color label, hangtag, color box & shipping mark。

这样一来，就非常清晰明了，一旦客户要整理这些东西，只要根据主题新建不同的文件夹，然后每封邮件里的附件都另存到这个文件夹里，就很有条理，也节省对方时间。

这比起一封邮件里，一股脑儿塞一大堆附件，看得人头昏脑涨，明显要好得多。其实在回复询盘和日常的邮件往来里，都可以用到这些细节，它们看似简单，却是大家最容易忽视的地方。这种邮件的分类发送，跟笔者过去提出的开发信 Mail Group（邮件群）的方法异曲同工。（具体可参阅拙作《外贸高手客户成交技巧》，中国海关出版社。）

102 图片的问题 Photo Issue

图片是个很重要的东西，很多时候比邮件本身的内容还重要。一张好的图片，也许能瞬间表达出几段文字都无法讲清楚的内容。而且图片拍摄的好坏，处理的好坏，也会直接影响客户对产品的感觉，对供应商的判断。

图片上可以加注

图片不仅仅是图片，起到的作用不只是描述产品，而是要把产品本身无法用文字表达清楚的地方在图片里体现出来。

案例 10-1 图片上的尺寸表述

举个例子，一个马克杯，要描述详细的尺寸给客人，如果用文字表述，要写上边的直径多少，下边的直径多少，高度多少，壁厚多少，手柄外侧尺寸多少，内侧尺寸多少等。如果碰到这个杯子是啤酒桶形状的，那就更麻烦了，每一段的尺寸都要用文字表述，不仅业务员觉得累人，客户也觉得不可思议。对着一大堆的数字，客户很难在脑子里把它们跟实物完全对应起来。

但是一张好的图片就不同了，完全可以拍产品侧视、俯视以及底部的图片，然后通过箭头和虚线，把尺寸直接标注在图片上，然后几张图片合成为一张，客户一看，一目了然，什么都清楚了。

尽量用常规格式的图片文件

大部分客户都不是设计师或者专业的图片处理人员，电脑里都只能打开 jpg 和 pdf 格式的文件。也许对方没有 illustrator，也没有 photoshop，更没有 coral draw，所以，你要为对方设想，发送图片的时候，导成 jpg 或 pdf 格式再发，会节省彼此很多时间。

327

当然，有些用作印刷的文档，制作完成的时候就是 ai 或者 psd 格式，你如果要发送这类格式的文件，就需要同时附上生成的 jpg 或 pdf 格式文件，专业格式的文件给专业人士看，普通格式的文件给客户自己参考。

案例 10-2　给客户确认的图片文件

一个意大利客户给中国供应商下订单，采购 3,000 个园林割草机，客户有自己的彩盒设计模板，发了 psd 格式的文件给中国供应商修改，要求供应商加上条形码的信息、订单号码、出货时间等，然后发回给客户确认。

这个时候，业务员并不能确定意大利的采购人员能否看 psd 格式的文件，也许这个文件是他向设计部门的同事要的，他并不能打开。这时候如果业务员根据 psd 格式的模板，修改好相关信息，发回给意大利客户的时候，就可以提供两个文件，一个是 psd 格式的文件，另一个是由 psd 生成的 jpg 格式的文件，给对方确认。往来的邮件可能会是以下的情况：

客户写的：

Sandy,

Please find the artwork draft in attachment, and help to add the PO No., barcode, article number and supplier code.

Rio

业务员回复的：

Dear Rio,

Thanks for the color box format. Please check and approve the revised files in attachment, one in PSD

for mass printing, and the other in JPG for your
review.

We look forward to your reply soon.

Best regards,
Sandy

这样就能缩短邮件往来的周期，节省彼此的时间。不管对方能否打开PSD 这类非常规文件，把事情做细致一点，多为对方考虑一点，总是没错的。

若正文插入图片，附件应当同时发送

业务员在与客户确认很多款产品的时候，为了更直观地展示产品，往往会在正文里插入多张图片，然后把要写的内容放在后面。这样的确很好，不用让客户点开附件，还能文图一一对应，节省对方时间。可是这并不是万能的，因为我们无法确认，客户能够准确地看到你正文里的图片，因为不同客户使用不同的电邮软件，而很多软件是不支持正文中内嵌图片的，他看到的就是一个叉。

所以为避免这类情况发生，即便正文里插入了各种图片，附件里也应该备注，比如加上一个 excel 文档，把图片处理压缩好，像报价单一样，后面加上要说的内容。或者把正文里对应的每张图片，编辑好内容，把文字标注在图片里，也能一目了然。

既在正文里表述，又加上详细的附件，双保险总是更安全些。

图片必须重命名

用手机或相机拍摄图片后，导出时图片会自动生成流水号，比如 IMG1068，表示的是你手机或相机里拍摄的第 1068 张图片，这个文件名对客户没有任何意义，保存附件的时候，为了以后方便查找，他还要对文件进行重命名，非常麻烦。如果是许多张图片，那就无形中增加了对方许多工作量。

所以图片处理完成后，发送之前的最后一步就是"重命名"。如果是给客户发送唛头图片确认，那文件名就可以改为"shipping mark & side mark"；如果给客户发条形码图片，文件名可以改为"barcode draft"；如果给客户发送很多张样品间图片，文件名也可以改成"showroom-1""showroom-2"，按顺序下去。如果客户需要另存图片，就很方便，点几下鼠标即可，不需要再重命名，将来寻找的时候也方便。

103 邮件长短的问题 Content & Space Issue

写邮件，究竟是详尽更好，还是简洁更佳，这个问题见仁见智。有些客户喜欢长话短说，一句话能说清楚的就不用两句话，也有部分客户喜欢把邮件写得详尽，方方面面都考虑到。

但国际上的商务邮件往来，还是以简洁为主，有别于 20 世纪七八十年代的翔实、正式，越来越趋向于口语化和生活化。过于详尽的邮件固然能表达很多内容，但难免让对方不耐烦。你可以换位思考一下，一个客户每天也许要处理两百封左右的邮件，如果每封邮件都是长篇大论，估计没几个人能耐着性子看完，最多只是扫一眼，看看说了什么特别有用的信息，没有就直接删除。

简洁的邮件会有一个问题，如果你同时要表达很多内容，既要给客户报很多款产品的价格，又要根据客户的要求对公司做简介，还需要回答客户关于交期、样品时间、颜色、包装等的问题，实在没有办法浓缩。遇到这种情况，笔者的建议依然是分成几封邮件发送，每封邮件突出一个主题，直接、简单、一目了然，避免客户在大段文字里寻找自己想要的信息，节省彼此的时间。

104 签名的问题 Signature Issue

正常情况下，每封邮件的下方，都应该有书写人完整的署名，包括姓名、职位、公司名、公司地址、电话、传真（尽管传真的作用已经逐渐被电邮替代，但缺少传真号码，总显得不够专业）、电邮地址等。

这是一个专业的商务人士应该做的，以便客户或供应商在需要联系你的时候，可以在邮件里迅速找到你的联系方式，或者根据公司名和网址在网络上搜索相关产品信息。一个标准的邮件签名，可以用如下格式表述：

Kevin Liu

Sales Manager–Gardening Accessories

ABC Trading Ltd.

Room1208, Block 3, ABC Plaza, No.8 DEF Road,

Pudong District, Shanghai, China

Tel：+86-21-12345678

Fax：+86-21-12345679

Email：kevinliu@abctrading.com

根据欧美商务人士的习惯，签名里一般是不会添加手机号码的。因为这属于私人信息，而商务往来属于公事，所以一切的私人信息是要摒弃在外的。当然，对于供应商而言，为了方便客户找到自己，有急事可以联系你，也可以在签名里加上自己的手机号码。

也许有朋友会说，很多客户的往来邮件不设置签名。根据笔者的个人经验，一般不设置签名，通常有以下几种可能。

第一，写邮件的人职位非常高，跟阅读邮件的人处于一个不对等的地位。假设一个贸易公司的业务员跟国外客户的采购员在谈某个项目，双方一直有邮件往来。但是突然客户的上司（也许是采购主管或者大老板）插了一封邮件进来，更改数量，要求降价。这个时候，这个上司的职位是高于业务员的，出于身份的考虑，他往往就会只写个名字，因为他知道，你们都知道他是谁，没有必要再多说明。

　　第二，写邮件的人通过手机或其他便携电子设备回复邮件，没有设置签名。很多时候，客户都会在差旅途中通过手机或者平板电脑之类的工具收发邮件，这时候他往往就会长话短说，几句话表达清楚，也没有设置复杂的签名，甚至没有抬头，没有署名，就像短信往来一样。

　　第三，邮件往来的双方是熟人，大家都非常熟悉。这个时候，邮件书写会变得很随意，可以写多一点，也可以一两句话，可以不用抬头没有结尾，也可以两三个单词就算一封邮件。大家都熟知对方的情况和联系方式，邮件的往来更加简单，不设置签名用一个简单的英文名字就足够了。这就像英文中的正式和非正式用法，只有熟人之间才会经常用非正式的用语，因为彼此间的距离很近，关系不错，没有必要特别客气。

105 邮箱地址的问题 Email Address Issue

写商务邮件，要注意两个问题，一是邮件抄送的问题，二是发件人邮箱的问题。

邮件抄送的问题

首先，如果对方写邮件过来，你要先看清楚，抄送栏里是否有别的人被抄送到。也许一个采购员发询盘过来，但是邮件抄送了他的上司，如果业务员回复的时候，没有点"全部回复"，那就等于只回复对方一个人，他收到后，也许还要转一份给他的上司，那就非常麻烦，无形中浪费了对方的时间。

其次，如果回复的时候要抄送给自己的同事或者经理，就要记得在抄送栏里加上自己人的邮箱。很多邮件的往来不是双方的，而是多方的，所以一定要记得全部回复，抄送到所有的相关人士。

最后，抄送邮件给某人的时候，如果是手动输入某人的邮箱地址，而不是导入储存的联系人，就需要仔细检查，是否有拼写错误或者遗漏，以免对方无法收到邮件。

发件人邮箱的问题

有些公司有多个邮箱抬头，比如某某邮箱维护老客户，某某邮箱联系新客户，或者某某邮箱处理电器产品的询价，某某邮箱负责小杂货的生意，这就需要业务员通过 outlook 等软件发送邮件时，检查发送方的邮箱地址是否对应抬头的发送邮箱，不给客户造成误解。

另外，初次联系的客户，为了给对方营造出公司的专业形象，邮箱最好使用跟公司名字匹配的企业邮箱，而不是 163、yahoo、hotmail 这些免费公共邮箱，以免给对方带来不好的印象，甚至怀疑这个公司的真实性。在生意往来中，要尽量多用企业邮箱。

106 格式、行文、空格、空行和标点
Format, Writing Manner, Blank Space, Blank Line & Punctuation

格式（Format）

写英文邮件，格式一般有两种，平头式和缩进式。平头式指每一段开头都顶格写，没有空格。而缩进式更像传统的英文信函，每段开头要空四个字符。如下文：

案例 10-3　平头式邮件模板

Dear Helen,

Could you please give me the offer sheet today ？ I have to check with my boss again for this order soon. Hope we could get deal.

By the way, please also advise your booth number in Canton Fair, and I will discuss with you about some new items there.

Thanks and best regards,
Lion

案例 10-4　缩进式邮件模板

Dear Mark,

Samples will be prepared soon. Please confirm

that you will pay for the sample charge this time.

Attached you could find the PI with our bank account.
Please settle the payment and send me the receipt.

Thank you！

Yours sincerely,
Candy Wang

以上两种格式在邮件往来中使用较多，尤其是第一种"平头式"，更符合现代商务追求便捷的要求，得到越来越多人喜爱，使用率相对更高。而缩进式在平时的书信或传真时，应用更加广泛。"缩进式"写法毕竟相对正式，如果前后再加上客户的信息和自己的签名，就是一封非常正式的信函。

"外贸函电"是包含"函"跟"电"两个部分的，"函"指的是"信函"，"电"指的是"电邮"，侧重点应该有所不同。

还有一种平头式和缩进式穿插的"混合式"，如本来使用缩进式书写，但中间引用部分用平头式，起到重点突出的作用，但这种格式使用范围不是太广，远远不如前两种使用频率高。

行文（Writing Manner）

英文的电邮主要包含三个部分，抬头、正文、签名。

抬头可以用敬称，也可以直呼其名，根据双方的熟悉程度来使用。如果收件人职位相对较高，一般还是称呼对方"某某先生""某某女士""某某经理"更加合适，至少不会让对方由于称呼问题而不高兴。

正文在段落上要分清，既不能某一段内容特别多，也不能头重脚轻。简单的英文邮件以三段为佳，第一段开门见山，第二段写具体内容，第三段结尾或祝词。正文的书写要尽量使用短句和简单的单词，不要为炫耀英文水平而使用冷僻词，也不要过多使用从句和长句，造成客户理解上的障碍。如何便捷就应当如何写。

签名尽量要补充完整，给对方留下专业的印象，也可以让对方在有需要的时候，第一时间找到你的电话号码等联系方式。

空格（Blank Space）

英文当中的空格是一个重要的细节，单词与单词间的空格，标点之后的空格，都会让一封普通的电邮显得更加美观。

英文和中文不同，中文的电邮，标点后面可以直接跟下一个字。但英文的标点使用的是半角符号，后面需要加一个空格，再接下一个单词，否则挤在一起，就影响审美了。试看以下的对比：

（错）Please do not forget to send me offer sheet,photo,manual and testing report.

（对）Please do not forget to send me offer sheet, photo, manual and testing report.

只是标点后的一个空格而已，但是视觉效果差异却不小。对比起来，孰优孰劣，一目了然。

空行（Blank Line）

英文书信和电邮中，空行是需要强调的地方，因为在传统的外贸函电里，要求的是段落与段落之间空两行，但如今，这似乎越来越不适用于日常的电邮往来，而慢慢演化成段落之间空一行。

至于传统的信函，还是以段落间空两行为主。

标点（Punctuation）

英文的标点，有几个地方是需要注意的。

首先，标点后空一个字符，再跟下一个单词。

其次，英文的标点中没有书名号，如果在电邮里引用某某杂志或者某某报纸，要记得用双引号。

再次，补充说明的时候，可以灵活应用括号、逗号，通过加注或从句的方式做补充说明或解释。

最后，要慎用感叹号。一封邮件里过多地使用感叹号，会让客户觉得你在对他咆哮或质问他，让人觉得你非常没有礼貌。

再版后记

再版的念头，其实多年前就已有。

那时忙着写新书，忙着做课程，忙着处理工作，忙着……好吧，我编不下去了，我承认，是我懒，很多事情习惯性往后推，就如同《外贸高手客户成交技巧2：揭秘买手思维》中的 procrastination，经常连我自己都看不下去。

但终究还好，我抽出了一大块时间，每天四到六小时，一页一页看过去，一句一句挑刺、修改，大篇幅重写，修正一些句型，选择更专业、更地道的表达方式，希望把初版中的内容，做一次大改动，用更好的方式来呈现外贸函电写作。让邮件本身更自然精致，多一些舒适，少一些匠气。

大音希声，大象无形。

毅 冰
2018 年 8 月 2 日
于杭州

书目介绍

乐 贸 系 列

书名	作者	定价	书号	出版时间
国家出版基金项目				
1. "质"造全球:消费品出口质量管控指南	SGS 通标标准技术服务有限公司	80.00 元	978-7-5175-0289-0	2018 年 9 月第 1 版
跟着老外学外贸系列				
1. 优势成交:老外这样做销售	Abdelhak Benkerroum（阿道）	45.00 元	978-7-5175-0216-6	2017 年 10 月第 1 版
外贸 SOHO 系列				
1. 外贸 SOHO,你会做吗?	黄见华	30.00 元	978-7-5175-0141-1	2016 年 7 月第 1 版
跨境电商系列				
1. 外贸社交媒体营销新思维:向无效社交说 No	May（石少华）	55.00 元	978-7-5175-0270-8	2018 年 6 月第 1 版
2. 跨境电商多平台运营,你会做吗?	董振国 贾 卓	48.00 元	978-7-5175-0255-5	2018 年 1 月第 1 版
3. 跨境电商 3.0 时代——把握外贸转型时代风口	朱秋城（Mr. Harris）	55.00 元	978-7-5175-0140-4	2016 年 9 月第 1 版
4. 118 问玩转速卖通——跨境电商海外淘金全攻略	红 鱼	38.00 元	978-7-5175-0095-7	2016 年 1 月第 1 版
外贸职场高手系列				
1. 金牌外贸企业给新员工的内训课	Lily 主编	55.00 元	978-7-5175-0337-8	2019 年 3 月第 1 版
2. 逆境生存:JAC 写给外贸企业的转型战略	JAC	55.00 元	978-7-5175-0315-6	2018 年 11 月第 1 版
3. 外贸大牛的营与销	丹 牛	48.00 元	978-7-5175-0304-0	2018 年 10 月第 1 版
4. 向外土司学外贸 1:业务可以这样做	外土司	55.00 元	978-7-5175-0248-7	2018 年 2 月第 1 版
5. 向外土司学外贸 2:营销可以这样做	外土司	55.00 元	978-7-5175-0247-0	2018 年 2 月第 1 版
6. 阴阳鱼给外贸新人的必修课	阴阳鱼	45.00 元	978-7-5175-0230-2	2017 年 11 月第 1 版
7. JAC 写给外贸公司老板的企管书	JAC	45.00 元	978-7-5175-0225-8	2017 年 10 月第 1 版
8. 外贸大牛的术与道	丹 牛	38.00 元	978-7-5175-0163-3	2016 年 10 月第 1 版
9. JAC 外贸谈判手记——JAC 和他的外贸故事	JAC	45.00 元	978-7-5175-0136-7	2016 年 8 月第 1 版
10. Mr. Hua 创业手记——从 0 到 1 的"华式"创业思维	华 超	45.00 元	978-7-5175-0089-6	2015 年 10 月第 1 版
11. 外贸会计上班记	谭 天	38.00 元	978-7-5175-0088-9	2015 年 10 月第 1 版

书名	作者	定价	书号	出版时间
12. JAC 外贸工具书——JAC 和他的外贸故事	JAC	45.00 元	978-7-5175-0053-7	2015 年 7 月第 1 版
13. 外贸菜鸟成长记(0～3 岁)	何嘉美	35.00 元	978-7-5175-0070-4	2015 年 6 月第 1 版

📖 外贸操作实务子系列

书名	作者	定价	书号	出版时间
1. 外贸高手客户成交技巧 2——揭秘买手思维	毅 冰	55.00 元	978-7-5175-0232-6	2018 年 1 月第 1 版
2. 外贸业务经理人手册(第三版)	陈文培	48.00 元	978-7-5175-0200-5	2017 年 6 月第 3 版
3. 外贸全流程攻略——进出口经理跟单手记(第二版)	温伟雄(马克老温)	38.00 元	978-7-5175-0197-8	2017 年 4 月第 2 版
4. 金牌外贸业务员找客户(第三版)——跨境电商时代开发客户的 9 种方法	张劲松	40.00 元	978-7-5175-0098-8	2016 年 1 月第 3 版
5. 实用外贸技巧助你轻松拿订单(第二版)	王陶(波锅涅)	30.00 元	978-7-5175-0072-8	2015 年 7 月第 2 版
6. 出口营销实战(第三版)	黄泰山	45.00 元	978-7-80165-932-3	2013 年 1 月第 3 版
7. 外贸实务疑难解惑 220 例	张浩清	38.00 元	978-7-80165-853-1	2012 年 1 月第 1 版
8. 外贸高手客户成交技巧	毅 冰	35.00 元	978-7-80165-841-8	2012 年 1 月第 1 版
9. 报检七日通	徐荣才 朱瑾瑜	22.00 元	978-7-80165-715-2	2010 年 8 月第 1 版
10. 外贸实用工具手册	本书编委会	32.00 元	978-7-80165-558-5	2009 年 1 月第 1 版
11. 快乐外贸七讲	朱芷萱	22.00 元	978-7-80165-373-4	2009 年 1 月第 1 版
12. 外贸七日通(最新修订版)	黄海涛(深海鱿鱼)	22.00 元	978-7-80165-397-0	2008 年 8 月第 3 版

📖 出口风险管理子系列

书名	作者	定价	书号	出版时间
1. 轻松应对出口法律风险	韩宝庆	39.80 元	978-7-80165-822-7	2011 年 9 月第 1 版
2. 出口风险管理实务(第二版)	冯 斌	48.00 元	978-7-80165-725-1	2010 年 4 月第 2 版
3. 50 种出口风险防范	王新华 陈丹凤	35.00 元	978-7-80165-647-6	2009 年 8 月第 1 版

📖 外贸单证操作子系列

书名	作者	定价	书号	出版时间
1. 跟单信用证一本通(第二版)	何源	48.00 元	978-7-5175-0249-4	2018 年 9 月第 2 版
2. 外贸单证经理的成长日记(第二版)	曹顺祥	40.00 元	978-7-5175-0130-5	2016 年 6 月第 2 版
3. 信用证审单有问有答 280 例	李一平 徐珺	37.00 元	978-7-80165-761-9	2010 年 8 月第 1 版
4. 外贸单证解惑 280 例	龚玉和 齐朝阳	38.00 元	978-7-80165-638-4	2009 年 7 月第 1 版
5. 信用证 6 小时教程	黄海涛(深海鱿鱼)	25.00 元	978-7-80165-624-7	2009 年 4 月第 2 版
6. 跟单高手教你做跟单	汪 德	32.00 元	978-7-80165-623-0	2009 年 4 月第 1 版

📖 福步外贸高手子系列

书名	作者	定价	书号	出版时间
1. 外贸技巧与邮件实战(第二版)	刘 云	38.00 元	978-7-5175-0221-0	2017 年 8 月第 2 版
2. 外贸电邮营销实战——小小开发信 订单滚滚来(第二版)	薄如骢	45.00 元	978-7-5175-0126-8	2016 年 5 月第 2 版

书名	作者	定价	书号	出版时间
📖 **贸易展会子系列**				
外贸参展全攻略——如何有效参加 B2B 贸易商展(第三版)	钟景松	38.00 元	978-7-5175-0076-6	2015 年 8 月第 3 版
📖 **区域市场开发子系列**				
中东市场开发实战	刘军 沈一强	28.00 元	978-7-80165-650-6	2009 年 9 月第 1 版
📖 **加工贸易操作子系列**				
1. 加工贸易实务操作与技巧	熊 斌	35.00 元	978-7-80165-809-8	2011 年 4 月第 1 版
2. 加工贸易达人速成——操作案例与技巧	陈秋霞	28.00 元	978-7-80165-891-3	2012 年 7 月第 1 版
📖 **乐税子系列**				
1. 外贸企业免抵退税实务——经验·技巧分享	徐玉树 罗玉芳	45.00 元	978-7-5175-0135-0	2016 年 6 月第 1 版
2. 外贸会计账务处理实务——经验·技巧分享	徐玉树	38.00 元	978-7-80165-958-3	2013 年 8 月第 1 版
3. 生产企业免抵退税实务——经验·技巧分享(第二版)	徐玉树	42.00 元	978-7-80165-936-1	2013 年 2 月第 2 版
4. 外贸企业出口退(免)税常见错误解析 100 例	周朝勇	49.80 元	978-7-80165-933-0	2013 年 2 月第 1 版
5. 生产企业出口退(免)税常见错误解析 115 例	周朝勇	49.80 元	978-7-80165-901-9	2013 年 1 月第 1 版
6. 外汇核销指南	陈文培等	22.00 元	978-7-80165-824-1	2011 年 8 月第 1 版
7. 外贸企业出口退税操作手册	中国出口退税咨询网	42.00 元	978-7-80165-818-0	2011 年 5 月第 1 版
8. 生产企业免抵退税从入门到精通	中国出口退税咨询网	98.00 元	978-7-80165-695-7	2010 年 1 月第 1 版
9. 出口涉税会计实务精要(《外贸会计实务精要》第二版)	龙博客工作室	32.00 元	978-7-80165-660-5	2009 年 9 月第 2 版
📖 **专业报告子系列**				
1. 国际工程风险管理	张 燎	1980.00 元	978-7-80165-708-4	2010 年 1 月第 1 版
2. 涉外型企业海关事务风险管理报告	《涉外型企业海关事务风险管理报告》研究小组	1980.00 元	978-7-80165-666-7	2009 年 10 月第 1 版
📖 **外贸企业管理子系列**				
1. 外贸经理人的 MBA	毅 冰	55.00 元	978-7-5175-0305-7	2018 年 10 月第 1 版
2. 小企业做大外贸的制胜法则——职业外贸经理人带队伍手记	胡伟锋	35.00 元	978-7-5175-0071-1	2015 年 7 月第 1 版
3. 小企业做大外贸的四项修炼	胡伟锋	26.00 元	978-7-80165-673-5	2010 年 1 月第 1 版

书名	作者	定价	书号	出版时间

国际贸易金融子系列

1. 国际结算单证热点疑义相与析	天九湾贸易金融研究汇	55.00 元	978-7-5175-0292-0	2018 年 9 月第 1 版
2. 国际结算与贸易融资实务（第二版）	李华根	55.00 元	978-7-5175-0252-4	2018 年 3 月第 1 版
3. 信用证风险防范与纠纷处理技巧	李道金	45.00 元	978-7-5175-0079-7	2015 年 10 月第 1 版
4. 国际贸易金融服务全程通（第二版）	郭党怀 张丽君 张贝	43.00 元	978-7-80165-864-7	2012 年 1 月第 2 版
5. 国际结算与贸易融资实务	李华根	42.00 元	978-7-80165-847-0	2011 年 12 月第 1 版

毅冰谈外贸子系列

毅冰私房英语书 ——七天秀出外贸口语	毅 冰	35.00 元	978-7-80165-965-1	2013 年 9 月第 1 版

"创新型"跨境电商实训教材

跨境电子商务概论与实践	冯晓宁	48.00 元	978-7-5175-0313-2	2019 年 1 月第 1 版

"实用型"报关与国际货运专业教材

1. 集装箱班轮运输与管理实务	林益松	48.00 元	978-7-5175-0339-2	2019 年 3 月第 1 版
2. 航空货运代理实务(第二版)	杨鹏强	55.00 元	978-7-5175-0336-1	2019 年 1 月第 2 版
3. 进出口商品归类实务（第三版）	林 青	48.00 元	978-7-5175-0251-7	2018 年 3 月第 3 版
4. e 时代报关实务	王 云	40.00 元	978-7-5175-0142-8	2016 年 6 月第 1 版
5. 供应链管理实务	张远昌	48.00 元	978-7-5175-0051-3	2015 年 4 月第 1 版
6. 电子口岸实务(第二版)	林青	35.00 元	978-7-5175-0027-8	2014 年 6 月第 2 版
7. 报检实务(第二版)	孔德民	38.00 元	978-7-80165-999-6	2014 年 3 月第 2 版
8. 现代关税实务(第二版)	李 齐	35.00 元	978-7-80165-862-3	2012 年 1 月第 2 版
9. 国际贸易单证实务(第二版)	丁行政	45.00 元	978-7-80165-855-5	2012 年 1 月第 2 版
10. 报关实务(第三版)	杨鹏强	45.00 元	978-7-80165-825-8	2011 年 9 月第 3 版
11. 海关概论(第二版)	王意家	36.00 元	978-7-80165-805-0	2011 年 4 月第 2 版
12. 国际货运代理操作实务	杨鹏强	45.00 元	978-7-80165-709-1	2010 年 1 月第 1 版

"精讲型"国际贸易核心课程教材

1. 国际贸易实务精讲(第七版)	田运银	49.50 元	978-7-5175-0260-9	2018 年 4 月第 7 版

	书名	作者	定价	书号	出版时间
2.	国际货运代理实务精讲(第二版)	杨占林 汤 兴 官敏发	48.00 元	978-7-5175-0147-3	2016 年 8 月第 2 版
3.	海关法教程(第三版)	刘达芳	45.00 元	978-7-5175-0113-8	2016 年 4 月第 3 版
4.	国际电子商务实务精讲(第二版)	冯晓宁	45.00 元	978-7-5175-0092-6	2016 年 3 月第 2 版
5.	国际贸易单证精讲(第四版)	田运银	45.00 元	978-7-5175-0058-2	2015 年 6 月第 4 版
6.	国际贸易操作实训精讲(第二版)	田运银 胡少甫 史 理 朱东红	48.00 元	978-7-5175-0052-0	2015 年 2 月第 2 版
7.	进出口商品归类实务精讲	倪淑如 倪 波 田运银	48.00 元	978-7-5175-0016-2	2014 年 7 月第 1 版
8.	外贸单证实训精讲	龚玉和 齐朝阳	42.00 元	978-7-80165-937-8	2013 年 4 月第 1 版
9.	外贸英语函电实务精讲	傅龙海	42.00 元	978-7-80165-935-4	2013 年 2 月第 1 版
10.	国际结算实务精讲	庄乐梅 李 菁	49.80 元	978-7-80165-929-3	2013 年 1 月第 1 版
11.	报关实务精讲	孔德民	48.00 元	978-7-80165-886-9	2012 年 6 月第 1 版
12.	国际商务谈判实务精讲	王 慧 唐力忻	26.00 元	978-7-80165-826-5	2011 年 9 月第 1 版
13.	国际会展实务精讲	王重和	38.00 元	978-7-80165-807-4	2011 年 5 月第 1 版
14.	国际贸易实务疑难解答	田运银	20.00 元	978-7-80165-718-3	2010 年 9 月第 1 版
15.	集装箱运输系统与操作实务精讲	田聿新 杨永志	38.00 元	978-7-80165-642-1	2009 年 7 月第 1 版

"实用型"国际贸易课程教材

	书名	作者	定价	书号	出版时间
1.	外贸跟单实务(第二版)	罗 艳	48.00 元	978-7-5175-0338-5	2019 年 1 月第 2 版
2.	海关报关实务	倪淑如 倪 波	48.00 元	978-7-5175-0150-3	2016 年 9 月第 1 版
3.	国际金融实务	李 齐 唐晓林	48.00 元	978-7-5175-0134-3	2016 年 6 月第 1 版
4.	国际贸易实务	丁行政 罗艳	48.00 元	978-7-80165-962-0	2013 年 8 月第 1 版

电子商务大讲堂·外贸培训专用

	书名	作者	定价	书号	出版时间
1.	外贸操作实务	本书编委会	30.00 元	978-7-80165-621-6	2009 年 5 月第 1 版
2.	网上外贸——如何高效获取订单	本书编委会	30.00 元	978-7-80165-620-9	2009 年 5 月第 1 版
3.	出口营销指南	本书编委会	30.00 元	978-7-80165-619-3	2009 年 5 月第 1 版
4.	外贸实战与技巧	本书编委会	30.00 元	978-7-80165-622-3	2009 年 5 月第 1 版

中小企业财会实务操作系列丛书

	书名	作者	定价	书号	出版时间
1.	做顶尖成本会计应知应会150 问(第二版)	张 胜	48.00 元	978-7-5175-0275-3	2018 年 6 月第 2 版
2.	小企业会计疑难解惑300 例	刘华 刘方周	39.80 元	978-7-80165-845-6	2012 年 1 月第 1 版
3.	会计实务操作一本通	吴虹雁	35.00 元	978-7-80165-751-0	2010 年 8 月第 1 版